Ice-Age Hunters
of the
Ukraine

PREHISTORIC ARCHEOLOGY AND ECOLOGY

A Series Edited by Karl W. Butzer and Leslie G. Freeman

Ice-Age Hunters
of the
Ukraine

Richard G. Klein

The University of Chicago Press

Chicago and London

The University of Chicago Press, Chicago 60637

The University of Chicago Press, Ltd., London

© 1973 by The University of Chicago

All rights reserved. Published 1973. Second Impression 1974

Printed in the United States of America

International Standard Book Number: 0-226-43945-3 (clothbound)

Library of Congress Catalog Card Number: 73-77443

CONTENTS

ILLUSTRATIONS

TABLES

EDITORS' FOREWORD

Over the past decade there has been a remarkable interest in early man,
both in the academic world and among laymen. This interest has been apparent
both in the increasingly successful efforts of multidisciplinary excavations and
in the growing market for comprehensible texts dealing directly or indirectly
with man's prehistoric past and the legacy of our hunter-gatherer forbears. The
intensity of ongoing research continues to accelerate, despite the increasing
retrenchment of those governmental agencies that control or supply the vital
resources without which fundamental but apolitical investigations would be in
dire straits. All told, the growing store of information now has multiplied by
a factor of ten over what it was in 1960. Yet the number of publication outlets,
whether for preliminary reports, extended interim papers, or monographic final
reports, has remained nearly static over the past twenty-five years.

In any growing field, transmission of data on important work is unsatis-
factory even under optimal circumstances. But researchers, students, and laymen
alike have been, and continue to be, unduly penalized in regard to developments
in the interdisciplinary study of prehistoric hunter-gatherers.

The fragmentation of publication media along traditional academic lines
continues to preserve such distinctions as anthropology, geology, biology, and
geography. The few interdisciplinary journals such as *Quaternaria*, *Eiszeitalter
und Gegenwart*, and, more recently, *Quaternary Research* are geared to short
articles and remain unable to cope with the pressure of relaying new information

to a wide audience in a reasonable span of time. It is unhappily true that the most prestigious traditional journals continue to be governed by editorial boards or referees who sometimes fail to understand the need for interdisciplinary efforts and, in consequence, relegate such papers to lower priorities. As a result of such factors, descriptions of current research are scattered piecemeal over many different journals on several continents.

Overloading of the existing media, particularly those accepting papers of substantial length, has reached the point where delays of up to several years in publication of results have become an expected part of prehistoric research. Equally undesirable effects of this increased pressure have been overcondensation, with format and length often totally unsuited to the material involved. Some authors have resorted to regional journals in far corners of the world, making it even more difficult for other scholars to keep track of their work, and well-nigh impossible for students to profit therefrom.

Early man studies covering the broad spectrum of prehistoric hunter-gatherers from the dawn of human culture to the beginnings of agriculture are at a particular disadvantage in North America. The growing number of relevant field expeditions and excavations by scholars based on United States and Canadian institutions finds no sympathetic range of journals and, above all, no university or museum monograph series such as those forming a repository for intermediate and younger ranges of Indian archeology. Some of the most original and detailed paleoecological work being done on the Old World Paleolithic today is carried out by teams from the United States and Canada; but, in general, the results are published in European journals and serials since no comparable outlets exist in North America. Moreover, those European serials that handle monographic studies are generally open only to those working with or from the associated institutions, and then it is often several years before a work appears.

Crucial monographs and articles by European scholars most frequently appear in languages other than English, and usually publishers abroad require that manuscripts written in English be translated before publication. Translation obviously involves further delays and costs. Also, all too frequently the

foreign language reading capacity of native English speakers, especially
beginning students, is very limited, and much though we deplore this deficiency,
ignoring those students is no remedy for this situation. In any case, the
relevant sources are published in a dozen languages. Lastly, when monographs
finally do appear, they are often priced well beyond the pocket of the average
student.

It consequently seemed to us that there was a substantial need for a new
outlet for work of intermediate length focused on interdisciplinary early man
studies. It further seemed to us that such studies should be produced both
rapidly and at a reasonable price if they are to disseminate information effectively. It is our hope that this simple but direct format will prove itself
flexible, esthetically pleasing, and, above all, within the range of the
pocketbooks of students in prehistory who have chronically been deprived of the
comprehensive site or regional studies about which our discipline revolves.
Such a series would not replace the lengthy and detailed monographs essential
to complete descriptions of prehistoric research, but would provide a medium for
the rapid diffusion of briefer summaries of some of the most important results.

The purpose of the Prehistoric Archeology and Ecology series is, then,
to provide a new medium for important unpublished research that is of prime
interest for scholars and students in English-speaking countries. It is hoped
that over the next few years this series will see significant contributions to
interdisciplinary early man studies from all the different continents. And it
is our explicit intent to encourage the fusion of Old World data and technique
with New World method and theory. Such key issues as the debate over assemblage
variability, the growing interest in "open-air" research and site internal
localization patterns, the application of statistics to systematics, and the
introduction of ecological models are all either direct products of such a
union or have been significantly promoted by it. They have not come from
European excavators who happen to have borrowed ideas from the North American
literature nor from American excavators who happen to apply their methodological
tools to data found in European sources. Rather, they are products of truly
international and truly interdisciplinary research. While the results of the

synthetic approach are still not very abundant, they have already influenced not only most other fields of prehistoric archeology but also areas so diverse as social anthropology on the one hand and sedimentology on the other.

In planning Prehistoric Archeology and Ecology over the past two years, we have been greatly encouraged and have equally profited from the response and ideas of many of our colleagues, of whom we must especially single out J. Desmond Clark, Glynn L. Isaac, Mary D. Leakey, James R. Sackett, P.E.L. Smith, and J. Peter White. We are also grateful to the University of Chicago Press for undertaking this joint venture with us.

As the inaugural volume of Prehistoric Archeology and Ecology, we are pleased to present Richard Klein's *Ice-Age Hunters of the Ukraine*. This critical synthesis of hitherto undigested material focuses on a key region for studies of late Pleistocene cultural adaptations. Fully effective human occupation of a periglacial steppe was achieved in the Ukraine at an early period, and the regional cultural sequence is remarkably florescent even in comparison with elaborate developments in the region of southwest France--an area usually cited as central with respect to the growth of Upper Paleolithic industrial complexes.

Richard Klein writes from a perspective embracing much of the breadth of paleoanthropological research. His interests and competences are grounded as much in the natural sciences as in anthropology. Most of the source material he employs has been unavailable to many English speaking scholars, or at best available in diluted and distorted forms. The fact that the book was written for the undergraduate and intelligent laymen does not prevent its being the most authoritative treatment of the material it covers.

In his introduction, Professor Klein presents a well-deliberated treatment of the aims and limits of paleoanthropological research. He then proceeds to discuss regional Pleistocene chronology and stratigraphy, past and contemporary environmental settings, and artifactual and structural materials from the Paleolithic sites in question. His concluding chapter is both stimulating and innovative. The complexities of origins and development of Upper Paleolithic industrial complexes from earlier Middle Paleolithic substrates, and the displacement of Neanderthals by completely modern *Homo sapiens* are discussed in brief but comprehensive fashion. Klein ties the relevant paleoanthropological data in with Service's progressionist models of societal development, and discusses such intangibles as communication and intelligence among our prehistoric forebears, as far as the data will allow.

The book has several other noteworthy aspects. It is refreshing to find such clear discussions, in plain language, of complex phenomena as those Klein provides in his discussion of the evolution of landscape in the Dnestr and Desna basins (chapter 2) or his compact definitions of artifact types in stone and bone (chapter 4). His section on structural features, especially dwelling remnants from two Mousterian horizons and ten Upper Paleolithic localities, is most useful and unusually well-illustrated--by his own pen--and will be a boon to the serious student, since the evidence examined is scattered through a dozen different primary sources. Such features are more abundantly reported from the Ukraine than from any other region at a comparable time period and constitute a major characteristic of interest to students of early man. The area is also notable for the abundance, in Upper Paleolithic sites, of art objects, especially human figurines, and these, too, are well-documented and illustrated in the report. Klein's discussion of faunas from Paleolithic sites and their bearing on man's part in the extinction of Pleistocene megafaunas is also of special interest.

In conclusion, we warmly welcome *Ice-Age Hunters of the Ukraine* and trust that it and its successors will prove useful and stimulating to an appreciative audience.

KARL W. BUTZER and LESLIE G. FREEMAN

PREFACE

Traditionally, studies of early man have concentrated on artifacts and
on establishing historical (genetic) connections among the "cultures" they
represent. In this study, the artifact genealogy approach has been studiously
avoided, not only because a growing number of workers (including the author)
are questioning its theoretical foundations, but also because it is difficult to
see its relevance to anyone but a few highly specialized scholars. Of much
broader relevance and of special interest at a time when man-environment relationships are a topic of everyday conversation, is the question of how ancient
man affected his environment and vice versa. It is the question of cultural
adaptation to environment in the Ukraine during a crucial interval in human
evolution--the Last Glacial period--that is the focus of this study.

Several years of teaching courses on early man have convinced me that
American undergraduates find the subject exciting, particularly if the emphasis
is placed on paleocultural ecology and not on the esoteric details of artifacts
and their "evolution." While this is true, there are remarkably few sources
to which interested undergraduates may be sent for semidetailed examples of how
past culture-environment relationships are reconstructed. I hope very much that
this book will help offset this shortage. Although it is by no means intended
to be a general introduction to early man studies, I have attempted to make it
usable in undergraduate courses by defining and illustrating technical terms
that the average student is unlikely to know. I have also sought to highlight

those general problems in early man studies to which the specific data presented here are especially relevant. These include such topics as climatic change over the last 100,000 years, the extinction of many large mammals roughly 10,000 years ago, the contrast between the life-ways of Neanderthal man and early modern man, and the fate of the Neanderthals in relation to the origins of modern man. Insofar as the data presented here very definitely bear on these matters and have never before been synthesized in a comparable manner (in any language), I hope this study will be of more than a little interest to my professional colleagues in archeology.

Professors K. W. Butzer (University of Chicago), J. D. Clark (University of California), F. C. Howell (University of California), Hallam L. Movius, Jr. (Harvard University), and C. Garth Sampson (Southern Methodist University) kindly provided criticisms of an interim draft of this book. I am of course responsible for any deficiencies that remain.

1. BACKGROUND

Early Man Studies: Trends and Goals

Early man studies are undergoing more rapid change today then at any time since their inception in the latter part of the last century. When I entered graduate school in 1962, it was widely accepted that man's antiquity did not exceed one million years and coincided roughly with the beginning of the geological epoch known as the Pleistocene or "Great Ice Age." This sometime truism has now been totally discarded. Research conducted very recently in east Africa has shown that undoubted members of the zoological family Hominidae, human beings in the very broad sense, were in existence by at least 5 million years ago and possibly before (Bishop 1971). By at least 2.5 million years ago they were even making crude stone tools (Isaac et al. 1971). Research conducted very recently in higher latitudes has shown that the glacial phenomena whose appearance has been used to define the base of the Pleistocene may extend back not only into the preceding Pliocene epoch, but even into the late Miocene, as much as or more than 13 million years ago (Bandy et al. 1969; Denton et al. 1971). Both the definition of the Plio-Pleistocene boundary and its relevance--if any-- for early man studies are presently unresolved.

In addition to far-reaching changes in the factual bases of early man studies, there have recently been important changes in underlying assumptions and goals. We no longer proceed on the assumption that virtually all observable differences among hominid fossils have taxonomic significance. The application of modern taxonomic principles which allow for reasonable amounts of intrageneric

1

and intraspecific variability has not only significantly reduced the number of recognized hominid genera and species, but has also increased the probability that the ones which are recognized are actual evolutionary units. The definition of such units is obviously essential to the goal of understanding how and why human evolution took the course it did.

There have also been important changes in the way we look at the cultural remains of early man. Older studies which emphasized historical sequences of stone artifacts have been increasingly supplanted by studies which emphasize past man-environment relationships. This is an exceedingly healthy trend, if for no other reason than that it is more to the point. In the older studies, stone artifacts tended to beget stone artifacts, and the people got lost; in the more recent studies, we are directly attacking the question of the origins and development of our present place in nature.

It stands to reason that modern early man studies are and must be interdisciplinary. It is obviously impossible to understand past man-environment relationships without adequate information on past environments. Even for the fairly recent past, it is becoming increasingly evident that we cannot assume the present environment is the relevant one. The further back we go in time, the fewer assumptions we can make and the more we must depend upon natural scientists--geologists, paleobotanists, and paleozoologists--to provide us with environmental information. As the study of ancient man-environment relationships has gained in popularity, natural scientists have played an ever bigger role in research projects on early man. Increasingly, the biological or archeological anthropologists who organized such projects have had to acquire some training in the relevant natural sciences in order to communicate effectively with their collaborators. Some students of early man have even acquired enough natural science training to collect paleoenvironmental data of their own. Conversely, some persons whose background was basically in one or another natural science have turned their full attention to early man problems. I personally would like to see the trends involved here culminate in the creation of research and training centers where representatives of all the kinds of people who contribute to early man studies could be housed under one roof. Obviously, such centers

could also include at least some of the geochemists and geophysicists whose
research has made possible the absolute dates we now have for various paleoanthropological and paleoenvironmental phenomena. As has been the case until now,
where absolute dates are unobtainable, relative age information could be
supplied by the same geologists and paleobiologists who provide the paleoenvironmental data.

It is a major purpose of this book to convince prospective students of
early man not only of the utility and merit of the interdisciplinary approach,
but also of their own need to obtain interdisciplinary training. Insofar as
this book concentrates on the interdisciplinary understanding of a series of
important early man sites in the Soviet Union, I hope it will serve to make a
further important point. Many of the sites to be discussed here have been known
for decades; the relevance of the information they contain for an understanding
of man-environment relationships during the long interval of time known as the
Last ("Würm") Glacial period is obvious. Yet they have figured very little in
Western summaries of Last Glacial prehistory, primarily because the basic data
on them are available only in Russian. If we are ever to obtain a reasonably
complete and balanced picture of human evolution in the broad sense, it is clear
that more students of early man must learn to read foreign languages easily.
Alternatively, we must encourage at least some students to specialize in critical
summaries of the relevant literature in languages that most students do not
bother to master.

Early Man Defined

To this point the term *early man* has been used very loosely. In fact,
in the preceding discussion, it could have been read as *prehistoric man* with
little or no loss in meaning. In what follows, however, it is necessary to be
more precise. *Early man* is used from hereon to refer to man prior to the end
of the Last Glacial, roughly 10,000 years ago. This is a conventional usage of
the term and serves to set off men who were either different from us physically
(taxonomically) or who lived in environments which, over much of the world, were
very much different from any that have existed since. In addition, all known

early men, as defined here, seem to have depended primarily, if not exclusively, on hunting and gathering and to have lived in social groups whose maximum size and complexity was far below that reached in various parts of the world in the last 10,000 years. *Early man* seems to have had little more impact upon the landscape than many other large mammals. In fact he may be regarded simply as an increasingly important--although never very abundant--element of the earth's fauna. However, beginning roughly 10,000 years ago, as a result of a series of major cultural innovations, especially the development of ever more effective food production, man's role in nature began to change fundamentally. For many purposes, man in the last 10,000 years of his history is more fruitfully studied as a major geological force than as another large and interesting mammalian species.

Not very long ago, *early man* was synonymous with *Pleistocene man*. To an extent, this is still a permissible equation, since the end of the Last Glacial is also conventionally regarded as the end of the Pleistocene, preceding the Holocene or Recent. And although the base of the Pleistocene remains unsatisfactorily defined, most known early men, including all those to be discussed here, are fairly certainly of Pleistocene age. The difficulty is that some of the most recently discovered hominid fossils from several east African localities will almost certainly be assigned to the Pliocene if and when the Plio-Pleistocene boundary question is ultimately resolved. In fact, there are some who would argue that we already have reason to suppose that hominids were present as early as the late Miocene (see Pilbeam 1972:91-99, with references). The term "early man" as defined here is sufficiently imprecise to allow for this possibility.

The earliest unquestioned early man sites, of late Pliocene to early Pleistocene age, are located in Africa. The apparent absence of such sites in Tropical Asia is perhaps a matter of insufficient investigation; on the other hand, their absence in Europe and temperate Asia probably reflects the inability of the earliest men to live outside the tropics and subtropics. Much of the data on human beings living during mid-Pleistocene time -- a vaguely defined time interval whose beginning could be tentatively placed between 1,000,000 and 700,000 years ago -- still comes from Africa, but data from Europe and Asia are known and are relatively abundant for the later mid-Pleistocene. Clearly, during the mid-Pleistocene, men succesfully colonized middle latitudes of the Old World, and there is evidence to suggest that this was made possible by interacting advances in biological makeup, as reflected in increased brain size, and in cultural capabilities, as reflected in competency in big-game hunting.

During the late Pleistocene, beginning roughly 100,000 years ago, human biological and cultural evolution proceeded to the point where man was in fact able to extend his distribution into virtually all the environments he inhabits today. Among the environments he succeeded in entering during the Last Glacial (beginning some 70,000 years ago) was the "periglacial" zone that existed not far beyond the margins of the great European ice sheets. Abundant evidence for periglacial cultural adaptations has been preserved in Europe, in part because of favorable depositional and preservational circumstances created mainly by the proximity of the glaciers themselves, and in part because by at least 30,000 - 40,000 years ago, men had adapted so well to the European periglacial environment that they may actually have lived in greater population densities than any of their contemporaries and many of their successors. The remainder of this study will be devoted to a discussion of some of the most remarkable evidence for the periglacial way of life that has ever been recovered. This evidence comes from the part of Europe which we know today as the Ukraine.

Early Man Sites in the Ukraine

The Ukraine is a Soviet Republic bounded on the south by the Black Sea, on the southwest by Romania, Hungary, Czechoslovakia, and Poland, on the north by Belorussia (White Russia), and on the northeast and east by the Russian Soviet Federated Socialist Republic (map 1). The first early man sites in the Ukraine were recognized in the latter part of the last century. Since that time, approximately sixty important sites have been found, and new discoveries are still being made. Unfortunately, language barriers have prevented Westerners from fully appreciating how abundant and spectacular these early man sites are. Many of them have provided enormous artifact collections including remarkable art objects; some contain ruins of structures which are among the best preserved and

Map 1.--The Ukraine and its neighbors

most interesting ruins known of early man sites anywhere; and most important of all, as a group they constitute an extremely rich source of information on the remarkable set of cultural adaptations which late Pleistocene peoples achieved in Europe.

The spatial distribution of early man sites in the Ukraine is itself a potentially important source of information on past human activities. Map 2 gives the locations of all the sites that have provided evidence of early man in primary context, that is, in situations where there has been little or no disturbance since early man departed. At all such sites occupational debris was covered by sediments shortly after site abandonment. In addition to primary (or sealed) sites, the Ukraine also contains several dozen localities where

Map 2.--Principal early man sites of the Ukraine and nearby areas. (Base map after Beregovaya 1960, map 3.)

artifacts have been found in secondary context (moved from their original positions) or on the surface (Beregovaya 1960: 15-16, 19-32, 104-55). Such sites have been largely ignored here because it is very difficult to determine how old they are and whether or not their contents are mixed, that is, derived from multiple occupations by people of different cultures over a long period. For present purposes, it is sufficient to note that the distribution pattern of secondary and surface sites tends to mirror that of the primary sites shown in map 2. The only additional important piece of information the surface and secondary sites provide is direct proof that the sealed localities represent only a fraction of the total number of sites early man actually occupied.

As map 2 shows, the primary sites are concentrated in the valleys of the great rivers of the Ukraine or in the valleys of their tributaries. Sites are especially well known in the valleys of the Dnestr and Dnepr rivers and along the Desna, a major tributary of the Dnepr. Important sites have also been found on the portions of these rivers or their tributaries that lie just outside the Ukraine in various neighboring regions. These sites have been included in the discussion here since the river valleys certainly constitute more natural units for the study of past man-land relationships than the politically defined Ukraine.

It is no accident that nearly all the known sites are situated in the valleys of major watercourses. Not only are these places which early man probably frequented, but they are also places which are relatively accessible to modern prehistorians and in which conditions of sedimentation (alluviation and colluviation--see chapter 2) have favored the preservation of ancient occupation sites. Moreover, the valleys abound in natural and man-made cuttings, and nearly all the known sites were found during examination of such "sections." Many discoveries were essentially fortuitous, resulting from the digging of a brickyard or cellar. For the reasons that have been cited, it is highly probable that the overwhelming majority of sites to be discovered in the future will also be found in major river valleys. In this context, it is relevant to point out that in many other well-investigated parts of Eurasia, known sites also tend to concentrate in river valleys, and for the very same reasons.

Since large portions of the Ukrainian river valleys have never been systematically searched for early man sites, the distribution shown in Map 2 does not necessarily reflect the distribution of prehistoric populations. Quite to the contrary, it more closely reflects the distribution of interested pre-historians and of the modern economic activity that facilitated site discovery. The distribution shown in map 2 may also be misleading because it only includes sites with large quantities of cultural debris. Theoretically, such sites could represent either places where animals were killed repeatedly or places where people camped for long periods. In fact, nearly all of the known Ukrainian sites seem to be long-term or frequently revisited campsites, which is not to say that they were not located near favored hunting places. Kill-sites of single animals and transitory campsites do not seem to be represented at all. In part, this is probably due to the fact that such sites contain comparatively little to catch the eye of the brickyard manager or even of the professional archeologist. Moreover, the very exposure of such a site may be sufficient to destroy it, or to transform it into a far less meaningful surface occurrence. And in a region where there are so many extraordinarily rich early man sites, the poorer ones may simply be judged unworthy of investigation.

2. GEOLOGY AND GEOLOGICAL ANTIQUITY
OF THE EARLY MAN SITES

Introduction: River Terraces

Each of the river valleys in which early man sites have been found in the Ukraine and nearby regions is characterized by a series of conspicuous geomorphic features known as terraces. These occur in step-like fashion up the sides of the valleys and represent stages in their development. Each terrace was formed when a river ceased to deposit alluvium at the level of the terrace and began instead to deepen its bed to some new level. Ordinarily, the greater the height of a terrace above the modern floodplain, the older the terrace alluvium, although this is not invariably true. Instances are known where alluvium of a more recent terrace developed to such a thickness that it completely buried an older terrace. Such a case exists in the Desna river basin and will be discussed below.

Most, if not all, of the terraces that are visible along Ukrainian rivers date from the Pleistocene. Terrace formation during the Pleistocene was encouraged by repeated changes in flow volumes and sediment loads, as well as in river-bed gradients. Variation in gradients was mainly a result of eustatic fluctuations in the level of the Black Sea, into which the rivers flow. During glacial intervals, when a great deal of water was locked up in the ice sheets, the level of the Black Sea fell, increasing gradients and encouraging downcutting by the rivers. During interglacials, the level of the Black Sea rose, decreasing gradients and encouraging valley filling. Locally, as for example along the Dnestr, crustal movement (uplift and subsidence) during the Pleistocene also

10

affected gradients, and with them, the likelihood that a river would be cutting or filling at any given time. The volume of water and the sediment load carried by streams varied with changes in climate. Generally speaking, more water or less load encouraged downcutting; less water or more load encouraged valley filling.

Changes in water volume, in sediment load, and in gradient did not necessarily occur simultaneously on all Ukrainian rivers. While some rivers were depositing alluvium along their banks, others were actively deepening their beds. In other words, terraces on different rivers are not necessarily in phase with one another. In fact, terraces on different segments of the same river need not be in phase with one another. In some cases, a change in climate seems to have induced alluviation upstream, while a drop in sea level led to downcutting near the mouth.

Most of the terraces that have been observed along Ukrainian rivers have only been dated tentatively. Precise age determination is complicated by the fact that erosion long ago removed long stretches of some terraces so that today they are preserved only as unconnected patches. Age estimation is further complicated by the mantles of nonalluvial slope deposits that tend to mask the topographic expression of terraces, making it difficult to identify them. These slope deposits are important in their own right, since they contain traces of early man even more frequently than does the underlying terrace alluvium, suggesting that most of the known Ukrainian sites were located on the slopes of valleys rather than on their floodplains. Early man's desire for well-drained camps may be the reason for this. Of course, even in cases where a site occurs in slope deposits covering a terrace, knowledge of the age of the terrace is important. This is because it will permit a statement about the maximum age of the site, that is, the time before which it could not have been occupied.

Earliest Man in the Ukraine

At present, the earliest undoubted evidence for early man in the Ukraine (or for that matter anywhere in the European part of the USSR) comes from terrace deposits dating from the earlier part of the Upper Pleistocene or, more precisely, from the Last ("Riss-Würm") Interglacial (table 1). Lower and Middle Pleistocene deposits are known in the Ukraine and environs and have sometimes provided remains of fossil mammals (see, for example, Aleksandrova et al. 1971), but so far pre-Last Interglacial evidence for man is restricted to some supposedly old-looking artifacts found in undated contexts or, more frequently, on the surface (Klein 1966b; Ivanova 1969c). The most promising among these are some crude artifacts which A. P. Chernysh (1965:21) found on the surface of the third terrace above the Dnestr floodplain near the village of Vykhvatintsy (map 2). It is unclear from Chernysh's publication whether any of these pieces were actually found in situ in terrace gravels. If they were, they would be no younger than the Penultimate ("Riss") Glacial, the terminal interval of the Middle Pleistocene as this term is used here (table 1). This is because it is highly probable that alluvium of the third terrace accumulated in this interval.

It is possible to argue that the absence of concrete evidence for Lower and Middle Pleistocene man in the Ukraine (and elsewhere in the USSR) is simply a result of inadequate investigation. Investigation has been sufficient, however, to document one important point: If man was present in the Ukraine prior to the Last Interglacial, he was not making hand axes and was therefore not part of the great Acheulean cultural tradition (Howell 1966; Collins 1969, both with references) which occupied Africa, parts of Asia, and western Europe during mid-Pleistocene times. Undoubted Acheulean hand axes are unknown from the Ukraine (and indeed from anywhere in the European USSR), even as surface finds. To the west of the Ukraine, hand axes in significant numbers and in primary context are known no closer than Germany (Valoch 1968, 1971). They occur somewhat closer as sporadic surface finds in Poland and Czechoslovakia (Valoch 1971). To the south they are found no nearer than the north slope of the Caucasus Mountains (Klein 1966b; Ivanova 1969c), while they are absent altogether to the east (Klein 1971).

Although occupation by hand ax-making Acheulians can be ruled out, the possibility that the Ukraine was inhabited by non-hand ax peoples fairly early in the Pleistocene is suggested by the occurrence of important Middle Pleistocene sites in neighboring countries. Especially noteworthy are Stránská skála and Přezletice in Czechoslovakia (Musil and Valoch 1968; Valoch 1971) and Buda-Varhégy

Table 1

Middle and Upper Pleistocene Stratigraphy of Middle Latitude Europe

Conventional Alpine Terminology	Britain (mainly after West 1967 and 1968)		Denmark, Nether-lands, and North Germany (mainly after de Jong 1967 and Wold-stedt 1967)		European Part of the USSR (mainly after Gromov et al. 1969)		PLEISTOCENE STAGES
							HOLOCENE
							10,000 B.P.
Würm Glacial	Hessle		Weichsel		Valdai		UPPER PLEISTOCENE
Riss-Würm Interglacial	Ipswich		Eem		Mikulino		±100,000 B.P.
Riss II Stadial	Hunstanton	GIPPING	Warthe	SAALE	Moscow	CENTRAL RUSSIAN	
Riss I-II Interstadial	Ilford		Treene		Odintsovo		
Riss I Stadial	Gipping		Drente		Dnepr		
Mindel-Riss Interglacial	Hoxne		Holstein		Likhvin		MIDDLE PLEISTOCENE
Mindel II Stadial	Lowestoft	ANGLIAN	Elster II		Oka	BELO RUSSIAN	
Mindel I-II Interstadial	Corton				Belovezhsk		
Mindel I Stadial	Gunton		Elster I		Berezino		
Günz-Mindel Interglacial	Cromerian		Bilshausen		Morozovka		700,000 (?) B.P.
							LOWER PLEISTOCENE
							±2,000,000 B.P.

This chart is included here strictly for heuristic purposes and no attempt will be made to justify the subdivisions and correlations. For this the reader is referred to the references at the head of each column and also to recent general summaries by Butzer (1971, chap. 2) and Flint (1971, chap. 24). It is important to point out that the Pleistocene stages suggested here are by no means universally accepted. Many authors subdivide the Pleistocene quite differently. It is also important to note that the number and status of the various Middle Pleistocene cold and warm units remains unsettled. It is entirely possible, perhaps even probable, that the "Mindel I-II" and "Riss I-II" intersta- dials were long enough and warm enough to qualify as full interglacials. In this case, of course, the "Mindel I," "Mindel II," "Riss I," and "Riss II" would all become full glacials. The Alpine terms are retained here because of their long-time usage, although the correlation between the Alpine glacial sequence and the other sequences is probably less secure than the correlation among the others.

and Vértesszöllös in Hungary (Vértes 1965a; Kretzoi and Vértes 1965). They are all dated mainly on the basis of the faunal remains they contain. These suggest an early to mid-Middle Pleistocene age, perhaps to the "Günz-Mindel" Interglacial for Stránská skála and Přezletice and to the "Mindel" Glacial for Buda-Varhégy and Vértesszöilös. Estimated dates of between 500,000 and 700,000 B.P. are probably of the right order of magnitude for all four sites.

At Stránská skála and Přezletice the artifacts consist simply of modified fragments of local rock not divisible into standardized tool types. Neither locality was clearly a human occupation site, and the principal investigators do not totally discard the possibility that the "artifacts" may be naturally fractured rocks. The presence of man at Přezletice is supported by a fragmentary molar which is believed to be human (Fejfar 1969). At Buda-Varhégy and especially at Vértesszöllös, there is no question about the artifacts being man-made. Vértesszöllös was fairly certainly a habitation site and contains bones of horses, bison, rhinos, carnivores, and rodents, at least some of which were brought to the site by man. Concentrations of burnt bone suggest the use of fire. The artifacts from Vértesszöllös and Buda-Varhégy consist of clearly modified pebbles (made into so-called choppers and chopping tools) and small modified and utilized stone flakes. Hand axes are completely absent, as they are at Stránska skálá and Přezletice.

Human remains -- some teeth and a skull (occipital) fragment -- found at Vértesszöllös are sufficient to determine what kind of man was living in eastern Europe in earlier mid-Pleistocene times. It was definitely a member of the genus *Homo*, though there has been some disagreement over whether it was *Homo erectus* (that is, a type of man similar to Peking man or Java man) or early *Homo sapiens* (Thoma 1967, 1969; Thoma and Vértes 1971; Wolpoff 1971). In fact, this may be a distinction without a difference since it is possible that the Vértesszöllös people belonged to a population transitional from *Homo erectus* to *Homo sapiens*.

Among countries bordering the Ukraine, sites of later mid-Pleistocene (post-"Mindel") age are known in both Poland and Czechoslovakia (Valoch 1971). The most prominent sites completely lack hand axes. Like the earlier mid-Pleistocene localities discussed above, the later ones are relatively rare, a fact which may be used to argue that traces of man may yet be found in mid-Pleistocene sediments in the Ukraine. It is relevant to point out that man would certainly not have been excluded from the Ukraine by the absence of game. This has been documented beyond all doubt by discoveries made in alluvium of the fifth terrace above the Dnestr floodplain near the town of Tiraspol' (Aleksandrova et al. 1971). This locality has provided remains of mammoth (*Mammuthus trogontherii*), horses (*Equus* aff. *süssenbornensis, E.* cf. *mosbachensis,* among others), rhinos (*Dicerorhinus etruscus* and *D. kirchbergensis*), camel (*Paracamelus* sp.), bison (*Bison schoetensacki* subspp.), antelope (*Pontoceros ambiguus*), moose (*Alces latifrons*), deer (*Praemegaceros verticornis, Praedama* cf. *süssenbornensis, Cervus acoronatus, C.* cf. *elephoides*), and other creatures (especially rodents and carnivores), which indicate an age close to that of Vértesszöllös. Although no traces of human activity have been found at Tiraspol', information on its absolute age has already made it a pertinent locality in discussions of early man. Paleomagnetic analysis of sediment samples from the Dnestr Valley have shown that terraces higher than the fifth (Tiraspol' terrace) all formed during an interval of reversed polarity (when a modern compass needle would have pointed south), while the fifth and younger terraces accumulated during an epoch of normal polarity (Pevzner 1970). This suggests that the fossiliferous deposits at Tiraspol' date from near the time of the last long-term change in the direction of the earth's magnetic field, some 700,000 years ago (Watkins 1972, with references)--hence the order of magnitude estimate for the habitation site of Vértesszöllös.[1]

A circumstantial argument that man might not have been present in the Ukraine (or elsewhere in the European USSR) prior to the Upper Pleistocene could be based on the observation that the Ukraine is and presumably always has been environmentally distinct from its western neighbors, particularly in the greater severity of its winters. The present day 0°C (32°F) January isotherm coincides very roughly with the Ukraine's southern and western boundaries. It is thus possible to argue that man may simply not have developed the cultural capability to live there until the Upper Pleistocene. It will probably be many years before

---

1. A roughly comparable age estimate can also be obtained on the basis of paleomagnetic data reported recently from the Netherlands (Zagwijn et al. 1971).

the archeological exploration necessary to discount or confirm this possibility
will have been carried out.

Upper Pleistocene Stratigraphy and Chronology
in Middle Latitude Europe

Insofar as all the well-documented early man sites in the Ukraine and
immediate environs date from the Upper Pleistocene, this interval of time must
be considered in some detail. As already indicated, it began with the Last
Interglacial, on the order of 100,000 years ago (table 1). This interglacial
(it was, in fact, an interval of varying climate--see chapter 3) lasted until
approximately 70,000 years ago, when it gave way to the Last Glacial.

Although a great deal remains to be learned about the Last Glacial,
research since the Second World War, especially in the last decade, has made it
by far the best understood segment of Pleistocene time. Studies in various
parts of the world based on change through time in such diverse items as sediments, pollens, and even insect faunas show that the Last Glacial was a climatically complex interval (Flint 1971:432ff.; Butzer 1971:274-75, both with
references).[2] For the purposes of further discussion, the Last Glacial may be
subdivided into three basic parts: early, middle, and late. To avoid the
awkwardness of terms like middle Last Glacial, the conventional Alpine term
for the Last Glacial, Würm, will be substituted for Last Glacial in what follows.

The early Würm begins with the onset of glacial conditions, probably
between 75,000 and 65,000 B.P., and lasts through the first peak of Last Glacial
cold, that is, until about 50,000 B.P. The middle Würm begins about 50,000 B.P.
and represents an interval of fluctuating climate lasting until some time
between 30,000 and 25,000 B.P. The late Würm follows this long interval of
fluctuating climate and includes the cold maximum of the Last Glacial. It ended
about 10,000 years ago with the return to interglacial conditions during the
early Holocene.

---

2. See also fig. 1, this chapter, which presents some current conceptions
of Last Glacial climatic history in selected parts of northern Eurasia. Studies
in Britain and the Netherlands have been especially thorough, as fig. 1 implies.

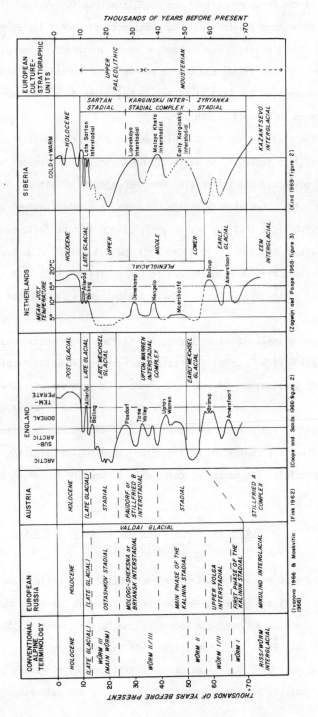

Fig. 1.--Comparison of current conceptions of Last Glacial climatic history in selected parts of northern Eurasia

In the European part of the USSR, the long interval of fluctuating climate known here as the middle Würm has not yet been fully recognized, although evidence for it exists. For the moment, most authors (for example Ivanova 1969c, 1969d, or Velichko 1969a) speak of a single undifferentiated interstadial (Mologo-Sheksna or Bryansk) of uncertain beginning date, and termination sometime between 30,000 and 25,000 B.P.

The distribution of Ukrainian and nearby early man sites within the Last Glacial is presented in table 2. Geological data have not been systematically collected and interpreted for the majority of sites. As a consequence, they can only be tentatively assigned to one or another segment of the Last Glacial, with sites that are not securely placed in time followed by an interrogation mark in the table. Detailed geological studies, allowing highly reliable age estimates, have been undertaken in two areas--the basins of the middle Dnestr and of the middle Desna. These regions are given special attention immediately below.

For a small number of sites, radiocarbon determinations allow corroboration of an age estimate established by other means (table 3). The relatively small number of available dates in comparison with the number on similar sites in western Europe is a reflection of the relatively limited facilities for radiocarbon dating in the USSR in combination with the considerable expense (the 1972 equivalent of $100-$150) involved in obtaining a single date. Almost certainly, the number of dates will be greatly increased in the next decade.

Geological Context and Age of Early Man Sites in the Middle Dnestr Basin

Perhaps the most complete and most detailed profiles through deposits of Last Glacial age in the USSR have been exposed at the early man sites of Molodova I and V on the middle course of the Dnestr (Ivanova 1958, 1959, 1960, 1961a, 1961b, 1961c, 1962, 1964, 1966, 1969a; Ivanova and Chernysh 1965). At both sites, the Last Glacial deposits consist chiefly of fine-grained colluvium, that is, sediment brought from upslope by gravity and rainwash. The colluvium

overlies the second terrace above the Dnestr floodplain. Near the mouth of the
Dnestr, alluvium of this terrace has been observed to grade into deposits of the
Karangat Transgression of the Black Sea, securely dated to the Last Interglacial.
It follows that second terrace alluvium must also have accumulated during this
interval and that the colluvial covering deposits must date from the Last Glacial.
At Molodova I, not only does the colluvium overlie second terrace alluvium, but
upslope from the early man site, the same deposits cover a thick fossil soil
(zone of weathering) containing shells of warmth-loving terrestrial molluscs
(especially *Helix pomatia*). Since this soil is also securely assigned to the
Last Interglacial, the Last Glacial age of the colluvium is doubly assured.

    The ultimate source of the fine-grained material (sand and silt) that
makes up the bulk of the colluvium at Molodova I and V is not totally clear.
It is probable that the material represents reworked wind-blown dust or loess
that was deposited over large parts of the European USSR during the Last Glacial.
The loess, in turn, was probably deflated from vegetationless areas immediately
adjacent to the great ice sheet that covered the northern part of the European
USSR. Subsequent to its deposition on slopes, loess was frequently subjected to
redeposition by water and gravity. The genesis of the material at Molodova I and
V may thus be difficult to establish.

    At both Molodova I and V, deposition of colluvium during the Last Glacial
sometimes slowed or ceased altogether. At such times the exposed surface of
the deposits was weathered and a soil was formed which was subsequently buried
when deposition began anew. The times of slowed deposition and soil development
are generally believed to have been warmer intervals or interstadials within the
Last Glacial. Substantiation of this notion may be seen in the fact that the
buried soils exposed in profiles through colluvium covering the second Dnestr
terrace never contain shells of cold-loving terrestrial molluscs (specifically
Vallonia tenuilabris and *Columella columella*), although such shells are common
enough in the deposits between the soils.

    The very steep slope of the locality at Molodova I meant that each time
deposition was renewed there, the soil that had been formed in the prior period
of nondeposition was seriously eroded. In fact, only two buried soils are

TABLE 2

GEOLOGICAL ANTIQUITY OF THE PRINCIPAL EARLY MAN SITES IN THE UKRAINE AND NEARBY AREAS
(Arabic numerals following the name of a site designate horizons within it)

	Dnestr Basin	Dnepr-Desna Basin	Other
LATE WURM (Upper Paleolithic)	Molodova V-1, 1A, 2, 3, 4, 5, 6; Molodova I-Upper Paleolithic levels 1 & 2; Ataki-Kel'menets I-1, 2, 3, 4; Chutuleshty I; Korman IV-1, 2, 3, 4; Voronovitsa I-1, 2; Ataki I(?); Ataki II(?); Babin I-1, 2, 3(?); Kasperovtsy II(?); Korman II(?); Korman II(?); Lis-ichniki (?); Oselivka I-1, 2, 3 (?); Oselivka II (?); Oselivka III (?); Rashkov VII (?); Rozhnev III (?); Rozhnev I and II (?); Volchkov 1, 2, 3 (?)	Avdeevo, Berdyzh, Bugorok, Chulatovo I, Dobranichevka, Eliseevichi, Grensk 2, Karachizh, Koromka, Kursk I, Mezin, Polduzh'e III, Studenets, Suponevo, Timonovka I and II, Yudinovo, Yurovichi; Dovginichi 1-4 (?); Dubovaya balka 1-8 (?); Fastov (?); Gontsy (?); Kajstrova balka (?); Kirillovskaya 1, 2 (?); Kladbishchenskaya balka (?); Klinets (?) Klyusy (?); Kulychivka (?); Lipa I (?); Lipa VI (?); Mezhirich (?); Noovgorod-Severskij (?); Novye Bobovichi (?); Oktyab'skoe (?); Radomyshl' (?); Yamburg (?); Zhuravka (?).	Amvrosievka (?); Bol'shaya Akkarzha (?); Glinyany (?); Bila (?); Min'evskaya (?); Prishivskaya II (?); Rogalik (?); Sharukanskaya II (?); Vladimirovka I 1-8 (?); Zamost'e I (?).
MIDDLE WURM (Upper Paleolithic)	Molodova V-7, 8, 9, 10; Molodova I-Upper Paleolithic horizon 3; Korman IV-5, 6, 7.	Chulatovo II, Pogon, Pushkari I, Gorodok II (?)	
MIDDLE WURM (Mousterian)	Molodova V-10B, 10A; Korman IV-8; Kasperovtsy I (?).		
EARLY WURM (Mousterian)	Molodova V-10C, 11A, 11B, 11, 12A, 12; Molodova I-Mousterian levels 1, 2, 3, 4, 5. Korman IV-earlier Mousterian levels (?); Osypka (?); Stinka I (?).	Kodak (?)	
LAST INTERGLACIAL (Mousterian)	Vykhvatintsy I (?).	Khotylevo, Negotino, Chulatovo III	

TABLE 2--Continued

Based on data in the following sources:

For the Dnestr basin sites: Ataki I and II (Ketraru 1969:71; David 1969:8; David and Ketraru 1970:32-33); Ataki Kel'menets I (Ivanova 1968); Babin I (Ivanova 1961b); Chutuleshty I (Ketraru 1969:75; Ketraru and Polevoj 1971:25; David and Ketraru 1970:29-30; Grigor'ev 1970:55); Kasperovsy I (Boriskovskij 1953:64-65); Kasperovtsy II and V (Boriskovskij 1953: 432); Korman I (Chernysh 1959:145); Korman II (Chernysh 1959:145-47); Korman IV (Chernysh 1970, 1971a); Lisichniki (Boriskovskij 1953:128-33); Molodova I and V (Ivanova 1958, 1959, 1960, 1961a, 1961b, 1961c, 1962, 1964, 1965, 1966, 1969); Ivanova and Chernysh 1965); Oselivka I (Chernysh 1968b, 1969, 1971b); Oselivka II (Chernysh 1968b); Osypka (Anisyutkin 1970); Rashkov VII (Ketraru 1969; David and Ketraru 1970:30); Rozhnev I and II (Boriskovskij 1953:135-36); Stinka I (Ivanova 1969b); Volchkov (Chernysh 1959:120); Voronovitsa I (Ivanova 1961b); Vykhvatintsy I (Sergeev 1950; Chernysh 1965).

For the Dnepr-Desna basin sites: Avdeevo (Velichko 1961a); Berdyzh (Tsapenko et al. 1961; Bud'ko et al. 1971); Bugorok (Velichko 1961a:151-53); Chulatovo I (Velichko 1961a:131); Chulatovo II (Velichko 1961a:125-29); Chulatovo III (Velichko 1969a:23); Dobranichevka (Pidoplichko 1969:64; Shovkoplyas 1970, 1971a, 1971b); Dovginichi (Boriskovskij 1953:147-48); Dubovaya balka (Kolosov 1964:46-47); Eliseevichi (Velichko 1961a:179); Fastov (Boriskovskij and Praslov 1964:31); Gontsy (Boriskovskij and Praslov 1964:31-32); Gorodok II (Boroskovskij 1953:145-47); Grensk (Bud'ko 1966:37-43); Kajstrova balka (Boriskovskij and Praslov 1964:29-30); Karachizh (Velichko 1961a:172-73); Khotylevo (Velichko 1961b; Grishchenko 1971); Kirillovskaya (Boriskovskij and Praslov 1964:31-32); Kladbishchenskaya balka (Zavernyaev 1970); Klinets (Nesyats 1957); Klyusy (Shovkoplyas 1967); Kodak (Gromov 1948:71-75; Veklich 1961:151); Koromka (Bud'ko and Sorokina 1969); Kulychivka (Savich 1969b, 1971); Kurovo (Polikarpovich 1968:196-98); Kursk I (Cherdyntsev et al. 1965:144); Lipa I (Savich 1968); Lipa VI (Savich 1969a); Mezhirich (Pidoplichko 1969:114); Mezin (Pidoplichko 1969:78); Novgorod-Severskij (Velichko 1961a: 134); Novye Bobovichi (Polikarpovich 1968:191-95); Oktyabr'skoe (Zamyatnin 1940); Osokorovka (Kolosov 1964:42-43); Podluzh'e III (Bud'ko 1966:35-37); Pogon (Velichko 1961a:150-51); Pushkari I (Velichko 1961a:141-50); Radomyshl' (Shovkoplyas 1965a); Studenets (Bud'ko 1968); Supnevo (Velichko 1961a:168); Timonovka I and II (Velichko 1961a:156; Grekhova 1968,1969; Grekhova and Sorokina 1969); Yamburg (Kolosov 1964:47-49); Yudinovo (Velichko 1961a:174-77); Yurovichi (Tsapenko et al. 1961:73); Zhuravka (Boriskovskij and Praslov 1964:35-36).

For other sites: Amvrosievka (Boriskovskij and Praslov 1964:23-25); Bila (Petrichenko 1963); Bol'shaya Akkarzha (Boriskovskij and Praslov 1964:27-28); Glinyany (Boriskovskij 1953:137-39); Min'evskaya (Boriskovskij 1953:369); Prishibskaya (Boriskovskij 1953:444); Rogalik (Boriskovskij 1953:393-95); Sharukanskaya II (Boriskovskij 1953:444); Vladimirovka I-1-8 (Chernysh 1953); Zamost'e I (Petrichenko 1961).

Table 3

Radiocarbon Determinations on Early Man Sites in the
Ukraine and Nearby Areas

Site	Date	Material Dated
Molodova V		
Horizon 1	10,940 ± 200 (GIN-54)[a]	Loam with charcoal
Horizon 1A	10,590 ± 230 (GIN-7)[b]	Bone
Horizon 2	11,900 ± 230 (GIN-8)[b]	Bone
	12,300 ± 140 (GIN-56)[a]	Loam with charcoal
Horizon 3	13,370 ± 540 (GIN-9)[b]	Charcoal
Horizon 4	17,000±1400 (GIN-147)[a]	Charcoal
Horizon 5	17,100 ± 180 (GIN-52)[a]	Loam with charcoal
Horizon 6	16,750 ± 250 (GIN-105)[a]	Loam with charcoal
Horizon 7	23,000 ± 800 (Mo-11)[c]	Charcoal
	23,700 ± 320 (GIN-10)[b]	Charcoal with ash
Horizon 8	>24,600 (LG-14)[d]	?
Horizon 9	28,100±1000 (LG-15a)[d]	Charcoal (base soluble fraction)
	29,650±1320 (LG-15A)[d]	Charcoal (base non-soluble fraction)
Horizon 10	23,100 ± 400 (GIN-106)[a]	Humic loam
Just above horizon 10B	>35,500 (LG-16)[d]	?
Horizon 11	>40,300 (GrN-4017)[e]	Charcoal
	>45,600 (LG-17)[e]	Charcoal
Molodova I		
Mousterian level 4	>44,000 (GrN-3659)[d]	Charcoal
Eliseevichi	33,000 ± 400 (GIN-80)[b]	Wood
Kursk I	11,600 ± 200 (GIN-94)[b]	Bone
Grensk-Horizon 2	20,750 ± 430 (LE-450)[f]	Charcoal

SOURCES: [a]Cherdyntsev et al. 1965. [b]Alekseev et al. 1964. [c]Vinogradov et al. 1962. [d]Ivanova 1966. [e]Ivanova 1969a. [f]Sementsev et al. 1969.

visible in the Molodova I profile, and both were severely truncated by erosion (that is, their upper parts have been completely removed). It is possible that other soils were destroyed altogether. Conditions for burial of old soils intact were more favorable at Molodova V, where the slope is less steep. Several buried soils are clearly visible in the profile as shown in figure 2. For the most part, they consist only of bands of humic loam, in one case severely crumpled by subsequent gelifluction (movement of waterlogged surficial sediment downslope over impermeable frozen ground below). But in one case, that of the

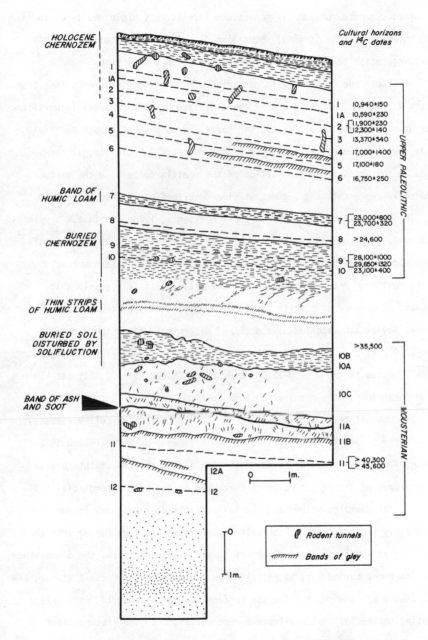

Fig. 2.--Section through the loams covering the second terrace above the Dnestr floodplain at Molodova V. (After Ivanova 1965, 1966.)

"buried chernozem" of figure 2, a nearly complete weathering profile is apparent. This buried chernozem presumably represents a relatively prolonged interstadial during which herbaceous (grassy) vegetation flourished in the area. This is the kind of vegetation that promotes development of such a soil type.

Although the relatively large series of radiocarbon determinations from Molodova V (figure 2 and table 3) is characterized by some internal inconsistency (stratigraphic inversion of dates), the series is consistent enough to aid in pinning down the geological antiquity of the deposits. Basically, it seems reasonable to suppose that the portion of the profile containing the various buried soils represents the segment of time described earlier as the middle Würm. The fact that the dates on cultural horizon 7, lying within the uppermost buried soil, have come out to only 23,000 B.P. or so need not contradict this notion. To begin with, the charcoal that was dated may have been worked down into the soil from the surface above; alternatively, it is possible that inadequate laboratory procedures resulted in dates that are "too young." Recently, Soviet laboratories have obtained determinations on the order of 28,000-29,000 B.P. on samples from horizons at Kostenki on the Don that were originally dated in the 20,000-23,000 B.P. range (Rogachev 1970:111; see Klein 1967 or 1969b:46 for the original Kostenki determinations).

It was pointed out previously that the middle Würm is believed to have been an interval of fluctuating climate. This is apparently reflected in the presence of multiple soils at Molodova V. The fact that none of them are as well developed as either the Holocene chernozem or the Last Interglacial soil (as found, for example, below Last Glacial deposits near Molodova I) suggests quite clearly that the warmer intervals or interstadials were cooler than the present, or at least of relatively brief duration. In addition, the disturbance of the lowermost buried soil by gelifluction, an erosional process that requires frozen ground at some depth below the surface, indicates that the intervals separating periods of soil development were quite cool. The preconditions for gelifluction are not met in the Molodova area today.

The deposits that overlie the portion of the profile with the buried soils presumably belong to the late Würm; those that underlie it may be assigned to the early Würm.

Figure 2 shows the stratigraphic positions of the cultural horizons of Molodova V within the Last Glacial sedimentary suite there. From the figure and from what has been said here, it is clear that the horizons referred to as Mousterian date from the early Würm and from the earlier part of the middle Würm, while those called Upper Paleolithic belong to the later part of the middle Würm and to the late Würm. The same chronostratigraphic relationship of these two major cultural units has been observed in various parts of Europe.

Since charcoal samples from the Mousterian horizons at Molodova V have proven too small and too old to provide finite radiocarbon dates, the absolute age of these horizons may never be known. I.K. Ivanova has attempted to date them more precisely by further interpretation of the early Würm deposits in which they occur. She notes that horizons 11, 12A, and 12 all occur in sediments that contain evidence of brief periods of soil development (weathering) under conditions of superficial waterlogging. These periods are recorded in the profile by clay-rich, mottled horizons known as gley bands, depicted schematically in figure 2. Ivanova has tentatively assigned these bands and the cultural horizons that are intercalated with them (11, 11A, and 12) to the Broerup Interstadial. In the Netherlands, this early Würm interstadial has been bracketed approximately beteeen 62,000 and 57,000 B.P. (see fig. 1).

The deposits that immediately overlie the gleyed sediments at Molodova V were crumpled by gelifluction, perhaps signalling the return to very cold conditions that followed the Broerup Interstadial. These geliflucted sediments contain Mousterian horizons 11A and 11B as well as a band of ash and soot that is widespread in the Molodova region. It apparently represents an ancient brushfire and is also well-expressed at Molodova I, 1.2 km downstream from Molodova V. At Molodova I, it also occurs in the midst of a geliflucted bed overlying nongeliflucted sediments with bands of gley. As at Molodova V, these gleyed sediments have been tentatively assigned to the Broerup Interstadial. At Molodova I, they contain all five Mousterian horizons that were found. The single radiocarbon determination from Molodova I, older than 44,000 B.P. on charcoal from Mousterian level 4 (table 3), does not contradict a Broerup age assignment.

Three Upper Paleolithic horizons were found at Molodova I. The lowermost horizon occurred in colluvium several meters above the Mousterian horizons, but slightly below the lowermost of the two eroded soils visible in the profile. It presumably dates from the later part of the middle Würm. The remaining two Upper Paleolithic levels occurred in fine-grained colluvium above the upper eroded soil. They apparently date from the late Würm.

Profiles comparable to those of Molodova I and V have recently been exposed in excavations at other sites on the middle Dnestr. At the site of Ataki-Kel'menets I, 8 km upstream from Molodova V, four Upper Paleolithic horizons have been found in colluvial silts and sandy silts above a buried soil complex that overlies more colluvium, in turn covering alluvium of the second Dnestr terrace (Ivanova 1968). The soil complex presumably belongs to the middle Würm; the Upper Paleolithic horizons may be assigned to the late Würm.

At Korman IV (U Mlinov), 4 km downstream from Molodova V, A.P. Chernysh (1970, 1971a) has found at least seven Upper Paleolithic horizons and several Mousterian levels in typical fine-grained colluvium covering the second terrace of the Dnestr. Upper Paleolithic horizons 1 through 4 occurred in sediments overlying a fairly thick buried soil and probably belong to the late Wurm. Horizons 5 through 7 occurred within this buried soil and may be assigned to the later part of the middle Würm. Two further buried soils, occurring yet lower in the profile, contained Mousterian levels which presumably date from the earlier part of the middle Würm or possibly from the early Würm.

At the site of Voronovitsa I, the colluvium containing two Upper Paleolithic horizons overlies the fourth terrace above the Dnestr floodplain (Ivanova 1961b:453). However, it continues downslope over both the third and second terraces and is structurally very similar to the silty sediments covering the middle Würm buried soils at Molodova I, Molodova V, Ataki-Kel'menets I, and Korman IV. It is therefore reasonable to assign the Upper Paleolithic horizons at Voronovitsa to the late Würm.

Geological data on the remaining Dnestr basin localities do not allow age estimates as reliable as those for the sites that have just been discussed. On the basis of the limited information available, the remaining sites have been hypothetically placed in time as shown in table 2.

Geological Context and Age of Early Man Sites
in the Middle Desna Basin

Thanks to systematic work by A. A. Velichko (1961a, 1961b, 1969a), a series of important early man sites located on the middle course of the Desna river and its tributary, the Sudost', can now be reliably placed in time. Velichko's views on the stratigraphic positions of these sites in what is generally known as the middle Desna basin are presented graphically in figure 3. His general notions on the Pleistocene history of this basin may be summarized as follows.

During the early Pleistocene, a series of erosional and aggradational events occurred which have not been and perhaps cannot be deciphered in detail. They left behind numerous erosional rills in the Cretaceous bedrock that are filled and overlain by relatively thin sediments of varied genesis. Some of these earlier Pleistocene deposits are believed to be glaciofluvial (that is, deposited by meltwater streams near the margins of ancient ice sheets). In places they were disturbed by frost action and sometimes they contain traces of buried soils. All this suggests that the earlier Pleistocene in the Desna basin, as elsewhere, was a climatically complex interval.

The early Pleistocene deposits are overlain by moraine (till) of the Dnepr ("Riss I") Stadial of the Central Russian ("Riss") Glacial. Traces of a soil formed on the till in the succeeding Odintsovo ("Riss I-II") Interstadial may still be found in places.

The Odintsovo soil is covered by glaciofluvial deposits assigned to the Moscow ("Riss II") Stadial of the Central Russian Glacial. The Moscow Stadial deposits are capped by a thick, buried soil, assigned to the Last (Mikulino) Interglacial and which may be traced northward to where it is developed on the Moscow Stadial moraine. Both the Dnepr and Moscow Stadial deposits are truncated in the Desna and Sudost' Valleys by alluvium of a "buried terrace" which is also believed to have formed in the Last Interglacial. At Khotylevo, Negotino, and Chulatovo III, this buried alluvium contains artifacts which are the earliest to have been found in place in the entire Dnepr-Desna basin. In fact, they

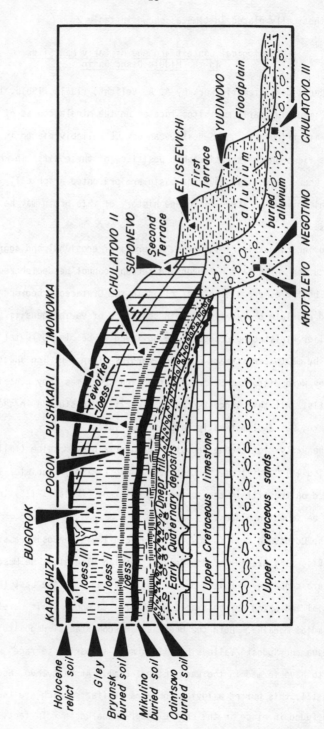

Fig. 3.--Stratigraphic positions of the principal Pleistocene archeological sites of the middle Desna basin. (After Velichko 1969a:23.)

constitute the best evidence for the presence of man anywhere in the European USSR prior to the Last Glacial. Their Last Interglacial age is supported at Khotylevo by shells of warmth-loving riverine molluscs found in the same deposits (Motuz 1967).

The onset of the Last Glacial brought an end to alluviation on the middle Desna and Sudost'. More or less simultaneously, fine-grained deposits (silts and sandy silts) began to accumulate on valley slopes. As on the Dnestr, these deposits seem to have been distributed by gravity and rainwash (as a colluvium), although they may originally have been derived from wind-blown dust or loess brought from the barren areas adjacent to the great ice sheet of the Last Glacial. In any case, Velichko refers to the fine-grained colluvium of the middle Desna basin as loess. As does that in the Dnestr basin, it contains buried soils believed to represent milder interstadials when deposition on slopes slowed or ceased altogether. Velichko has used these soils to subdivide the loess into three basic parts.

Loess I lies directly on the Last Interglacial soil. Relatively few exposures of it are known and none of them are very thick. It is capped by a well-developed buried soil which Velichko assigns to the Bryansk Interstadial. Loess I obviously predates the late Würm. It is possible that it spans both the early and middle Würm as defined here, although this cannot be proven with the information at hand. No archeological sites have yet been found in loess I, though it is likely that man occupied the middle Desna basin during the time interval in which it was deposited. This is suggested both by the occurrence of Last Interglacial sites, such as the one at Khotylevo, and by early Würm occupation sites on the Dnestr and elsewhere in the European USSR.

Three middle Desna sites--Pushkari I, Pogon, and Chulatovo II--have been found directly above the Bryansk soil at the base of loess II. The occupants of these sites may actually have walked on the surface represented by the Bryansk soil. The sites therefore may date from the very end of the middle Würm. They are the oldest Upper Paleolithic localities so far found in the Desna basin, though they are probably somewhat younger than the oldest ones along the Dnestr. At Molodova V, for example, the earliest Upper Paleolithic horizons--9 and 10--occur within, rather than on the surface of, a late middle-Würm buried soil. They therefore antedate the end of the middle Würm by some interval.

Perhaps somewhat younger than Pushkari I, Pogon, and Chulatovo II is the site of Chulatovo I. Its cultural horizon apparently lies within the body of loess II. It would date from the early part of the late Würm.

Loess II is separated from loess III by a weakly developed, buried gley soil. Its precise age has not been established, but it may be relevant that that bands of gley have been found within the late Würm colluvium of Molodova V between cultural horizons 6 and 4, dated to roughly 17,000 B.P. (see fig. 2). The soil between loess II and III may be of the same age. It represents at most a relatively unimportant oscillation toward warmer climate within the generally cold late Würm.

Loess III contains at least two Upper Paleolithic sites--Bugorok and Karachizh, both on the middle Desna. In some places, shortly after primary deposition, loess III was subject to considerable reworking and redeposition on slopes and in ravines. The fact that the reworking took place still within the late Würm (rather than in the Holocene) is clearly shown at the Desna sites of Timonovka I and II. At both sites the cultural horizons, occurring within reworked loess III, are interrupted by ice-wedge casts--features that suggest permanently frozen subsoil after the sites were abandoned. Permanently frozen ground and ice wedges are today found only far to the north of the middle Desna. Ice-wedge casts also interrupt the cultural horizons at other sites in the Upper Dnepr-Desna basin--most notably at Avdeevo, Berdyzh, Bugorok, Grensk, and Podluzh'e III--where they also indicate far colder conditions than obtain in the area at present.

Near the end of the late Würm, deposition of fine-grained sediments on slopes ceased, while at the same time the middle Desna and the Sudost' renewed active deposition along their banks. At least two distinct phases of alluviation occurred during the terminal part of the late Würm, resulting in the formation of two alluvial terraces. Alluvium of the upper or second terrace truncates the in situ loessic deposits on the higher slopes; this, together with the fact that neither terrace is covered by loess, indicates quite clearly that the alluvium of both terraces is younger than the loesses. Second terrace alluvium on the Sudost' contains the important archeological site of Eliseevichi, which accordingly should date to the very late Würm. Curiously, a wood sample from this site has been radiocarbon-dated to 33,000 ± 400 (table 3), an anomaly that still lacks explanation. The cultural materials at the Sudost' site of Kurovo also probably occurred near the top of second terrace alluvium, while the cultural horizon of Suponevo on the Desna was found in the fill of a ravine that grades into second terrace alluvium, a fill consisting of reworked loess III.

Finally, the Sudost' site of Yudinovo, and probably also the Desna site of Mezin, occur near the top of the alluvium of the first terrace. They presumably date from the very end of the Würm.

If, as Velichko and others imply, the scheme he has developed for the middle Desna and Sudost' may be generalized at least in part to another major tributary of the Desna, the Sejm, and also to the upper Dnepr and to two more of its principal tributaries, the Sozh and the Pripyat' (map 2), then some additional early man sites may be considered dated. These include Avdeevo on the Sejm; Grensk, Berdyzh, and Podluzh'e III on the Sozh; Koromka on the upper Dnepr; and Yurovichi on the Pripyat'. Avdeevo, Grensk (horizon 2), Podluzh'e III, and Koromka all occur near the top of first terrace body on their respective rivers in deposits of mixed alluvial and colluvial origin. Berdyzh and Yurovichi are stratified in ravine fills that grade into first terrace alluvium on their rivers. If the first terraces above the floodplains of the Sejm, upper Dnepr, Sozh, and Pripyat' may be correlated with the first terraces of the middle Desna and Sudost', all six cited localities would date from the very end of the late Würm. In at least the case of the upper Dnepr, however, generalization from the middle Desna may be premature since charcoal from the lower (second) horizon of Grensk has provided an incongruously old radiocarbon date of 20,750 ± 430 (table 3). None of the other sites has been radiocarbon dated, though the cultural materials found at Avdeevo are so similar to those found in level 1 of the Don River site of Kostenki I that a date on the latter may well apply to Avdeevo as well. This date, 14,200 ± 60 (GIN-86) on charred bone (Klein 1967), is more in line with a very late Würm age estimate made on strictly geological grounds.

Insufficient data have been published on most of the remaining sites in the Dnepr-Desna basin to allow secure geological assessment of their ages. For most of the sites, the estimates presented in table 2 must be regarded as tentative. Two exceptions are Kursk I, with a radiocarbon date of 11,600 ±200 (table 2) which may thus be assigned to the late Würm, and Dobranichevka. At the latter, the cultural horizon occurs in fine-grained sediments overlying a complex of buried soils in turn overlying alluvium of the second terrace of the River Supoj, a tributary of the middle Dnepr (Pidoplichko 1969). If the soil complex may be dated to the middle Würm, the cultural horizon may be assigned to the late Würm.

The sparse data available on the geological conditions in which the remaining Ukrainian sites occur, in combination with assessments of their arti- fact inventories, suggest age assignments as shown in table 2.

Conclusions

Table 2 is the principal conclusion of the present chapter. From it, several subsidiary conclusions may be drawn. First, all the sites securely dated to the Last Interglacial, early Würm, and early part of the middle Wurm belong to the Mousterian; all the sites securely dated to the later part of the middle Würm and to the late Würm belong to the Upper Paleolithic. The same chronostratigraphic relationship between these two major cultural units has been found wherever datable sites are known in Europe.

A second point is that, although the two major drainage systems of the Ukraine and nearby areas are about equally rich in late Würm and probable late Würm sites, one--the Dnestr basin--is far richer in early amd middle Würm localities. It is possible that the Dnestr basin was more heavily populated in the early and middle Würm. Certainly environmental conditions were somewhat milder there during these intervals than further east in the Dnepr-Desna drainage (see chap. 3). On the other hand, it is important to point out that known exposures of early and middle Würm deposits in the Dnepr-Desna basin are both fewer and thinner than along the Dnestr. This could easily be the reason why the Dnepr-Desna drainage has far fewer early and middle Wurm sites.

In this same context of site densities, it is obvious from table 2 that even in the Dnestr basin, most of the known early man sites are securely or tentatively dated to the late Würm. Although this may be an accident of preservation (younger sites tend to be better preserved and more easily found), at least equally likely is the possibility that it reflects marked population increase in the late Würm. Such increase may have been made possible by the extraordinary cultural adaptations that late Würm peoples achieved to an environment whose harshness was tempered by its comparative richness in large game.

3. ENVIRONMENT AND ECOLOGY

The Modern Environment

From a topographic point of view, the Ukraine may be divided into three principal areas: (1) a swampy lowland covering much of the area north of Kiev and passing northward into Belorussia on the west and the Russian Soviet Federated Socialist Republic on the east; (2) a great plain lying south of the swampy lowland and occupying most of the Ukraine; the plain slopes southward toward the Black Sea and is characterized mainly by low relief; and (3) the Carpathian Mountains and their foothills, located south of the Dnestr River, in the extreme southwestern part of the country.

The climate of the Ukraine is typically continental, with marked contrast between summer and winter. At Kiev, the January mean is a chilly -6°C (21°F), while the July mean is a warm 19°C (67°F). Even at Odessa, where the Black Sea might be expected to exert a modifying influence, the means are -3°C (26°F) and 23°C (73°F) respectively. Rainfall in the Ukraine is abundant only in the Carpathians, where it reaches values between 1000 and 1500 mm (40 and 60 inches). Kiev has a yearly mean of only 533 mm (21 inches), while the sea coasts rarely average more than 400 mm (16 inches). Precipitation tends to be heaviest in summer, which means that while snow may lie on the land continually in the winter months, it is rarely very deep.

Three principal types of vegetation occur in the Ukraine today, as may be seen on map 3, which shows the chief vegetation belts for the whole of the European USSR. In the north of the Ukraine and beyond its boundaries in

34

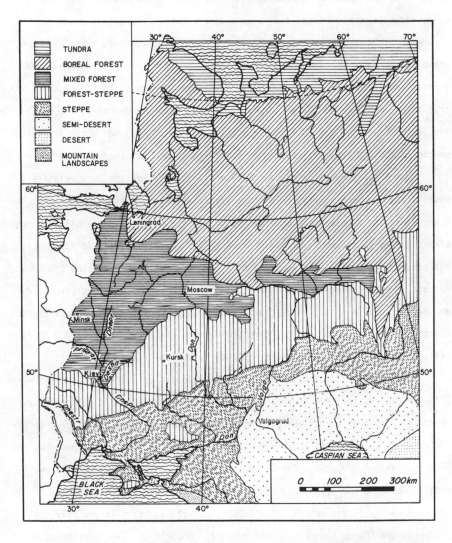

Map 3.--Modern vegetation zones of European Russia. (After Berg 1950:351.)

Belorussia and the RSFSR, coinciding largely with the swampy lowland mentioned

previously, is a belt of *mixed forest*, consisting of mixed stands of broad-leaved

trees, primarily oak (*Quercus*), and conifers, mostly spruce (*Picea*). In some

better drained sandy areas, forests of pine (*Pinus*) may be found. South of the

mixed-forest zone is an area of *forest-steppe* occupying the northern part of the

Ukrainian great plains. In this region, forests consisting largely of oak, ash

(*Fraxinus*), and hornbeam (*Carpinus*) alternate with treeless areas where herbaceous dicotyledons and broad-leaved grasses predominate. Farther south and extending right up to the Black Sea is the *steppe* proper, where trees are rare, except along watercourses, and the vegetation consists mainly of narrow-leaved grasses and species of *Artemisia* (wormwood, a close relative to sagebrush). The true steppe contains one large island of forest-steppe, somewhat to the north of the Sea of Azov (see map 3). This occurs on the Donets Upland, where increased precipitation and somewhat lower mean temperatures promote the growth of trees.

As a consequence of considerable altitudinal variation over relatively short distances, the vegetation of the Carpathians, in the extreme southwestern Ukraine, is too complex to depict on map 3. In the Carpathian foothills, forest-steppe passes into forests of oak, hornbeam, and beech (*Fagus*). At altitudes between 300 and 600 m (1000 and 2000 ft.), these forests are replaced by mixed forests of oak, hornbeam, beech, spruce and fir (*Abies*). The mixed (broad-leaf and coniferous) forests give way to more or less pure stands of conifers (spruce and fir) at altitudes of about 1200 m (4000 ft.). At about 1500 m (5000 ft.), trees disappear altogether and are replaced by subalpine meadow.

Until recently, the fauna of the mixed forest included European bison (*Bison bonasus*), red deer (*Cervus elaphus*), moose (*Alces alces*), wild boar (*Sus scrofa*), brown bear (*Ursus arctos*), wolf (*Canis lupus*), lynx (*Lynx lynx*), badger (*Meles meles*), and beaver (*Castor fiber*). It still contains fairly numerous roe deer (*Capreolus capreolus*), fox (*Vulpes vulpes*), and other small carnivores, such as stone marten (*Martes foina*), polecat (*Putorius putorius*), ermine (*Mustela erminea*), and weasel (*M. nivalis*), as well as hares--especially the European hare (*Lepus europeaus*)--and rodents. Roughly the same species occurred in the forests of the forest-steppe, where, in addition, the steppes not long ago supported fairly numerous saiga antelope (*Saiga tatarica*), wild horse (*Equus caballus*), and wild cattle or aurochs (*Bos primigenius*). A large rodent, known as the steppe marmot of baibak (*Marmota bobac*), was also once common in the grasslands of the forest-steppe. Finally, the steppe proper contained a smaller number of species than did the other two major zones, but the relatively large amount of edible vegetation within fairly easy reach supported great numbers of wild cattle, wild horses, and saiga antelope, as well as steppe marmots. Extensive cultivation of the steppe has eliminated all these creatures. Except for small rodents, the only major wild mammals found on the steppe today are roe deer and wild boar, still present in occasional woods near watercourses.

Sedimentological data, animal bones, and, above all, pollen found in Pleistocene deposits in the Ukraine and nearby areas show that for the most part early man lived under very different environmental circumstances than those which have just been described. With the modern environment as a backdrop for comparison, and, of course, within the limits of the available data, these ancient environments will now be described.

Last Interglacial Environments

Pollen diagrams from a number of localities have permitted Soviet investigators to reconstruct the broad outlines of environmental change during the Last (Mikulino) Interglacial (see especially Grichuk 1969a:45-52; 1969c:448-53). One of these diagrams, from the locality of Semikhody on the Pripyat' (see map 4), is reproduced here in figure 4 (bottom). As this figure implies, in the northern part of the Ukraine, the Last Interglacial was initially characterized by widespread pine-birch (*Pinus-Betula*) forests. Pollen data from the southern part of the Ukraine and adjacent regions indicate that to begin with, the Last Interglacial there was characterized by interspersed pine-birch forests and steppes. Subsequently, the pine-birch forests began to give way to broad-leaf forests made up chiefly of oak, elm (*Ulmus*), and hazel (*Corylus*). The importance of pine and birch was greatly decreased, although in the vicinity of Semikhody and other relatively sandy areas, pine, at least, continued to prosper. With the further passage of time, new broad-leaf trees appeared in the forests--especially hornbeam and linden (*Tilia*).

Hornbeam eventually became far more important than it is in the modern forests of the European USSR. The time of the maximum importance of hornbeam is known as the Last Interglacial Climatic Optimum, since it is believed that the extraordinary prominence of this tree indicates very mild climatic conditions--

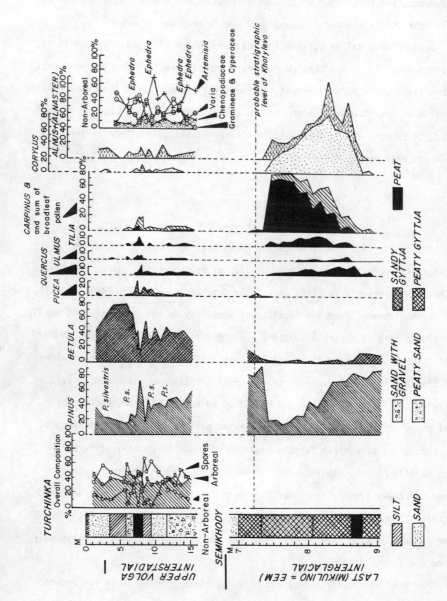

Fig. 4.--Pollen diagrams from Semikhody and Turchinka (Pripyat' basin). (After Grichuk 1969a, fig. 8.)

both more moisture and greater warmth than characterize the European USSR today.[1]
The logic behind this statement is that hornbeam today has comparable prominence
only in western Europe, where the present-day climate is for the most part
considerably wetter and milder than in the European USSR.

Sufficient pollen data are available from various parts of the European
USSR to construct a map showing the distribution of vegetation belts during the
Last Interglacial climatic optimum. Such a map, as drawn by V. P. Grichuk (1969a:
51), is reproduced here as map 4. For the Ukraine and its immediate environs,
the map indicates that only two major vegetation zones were present. In the
north was an area of broad-leaf forests in which oak, elm, hazel, hornbeam, and
linden were the dominant trees with alder (*Alnus*) important in the valleys. In
the south was an area of forest-steppe, that is, alternating broad-leaf forests
and grasslands. There was no true steppe. The implications of this vegetational
picture for human occupation are difficult to establish since there are no known
sites that clearly date from the climatic optimum. It is probable that game
was relatively abundant, especially in the forest-steppe, and fruit or nut trees,
such as hazel, were certainly plentiful enough to make them a potentially important food source. Although it must remain speculation until actual sites are
found, it seems likely that at least the southern portions of the Ukraine and
neighboring regions were occupied by man during the climatic optimum.

The climatic optimum was followed by a time of apparently rapid climatic
deterioration, during which pine and birch made a major comeback and were accompanied by spruce, which was widespread in the ensuing glacial. Pollen data suggest that Khotylevo in the middle Desna valley, and perhaps also Negotino and
Chulatovo III nearby, were occupied in the final phase of the Last Interglacial,
when climatic deterioration had already begun (Grichuk 1969a:45-46). Clearly,
climatic deterioration was no obstacle to human settlement, since as
was pointed out in chapter 2, sites of Last Glacial age are quite common
in the Ukraine and environs. In fact, as will be argued below, there are
reasons to suppose that during some parts of the Last Glacial, the Ukraine may

_____

1. Grichuk estimates a January mean for the northern Ukraine of 0.6°C
(33°F).

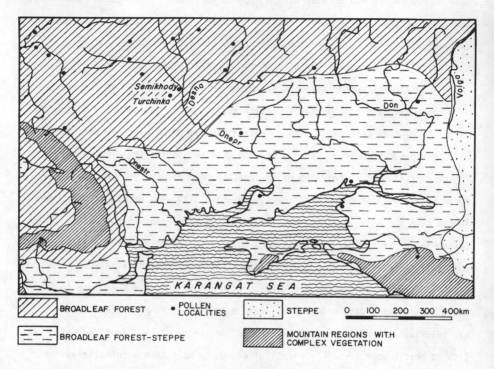

Map 4.--Vegetation zones of European Russia during the Last Interglacial climatic optimum. (After Grichuk 1969a, fig. 11.)

actually have been more suitable for human habitation than it was during the Last Interglacial.

Data from other sources, especially from buried soils, tend to corroborate the picture of Last Interglacial environments suggested by the pollen data. So, for example, Morozova (1969a, 1969c; also Velichko and Morozova 1969) points out that Last Interglacial soils lying roughly north of Kiev were clearly formed under forest vegetation, while both forests and grasslands seem to have played a role further south. She also indicates that the Last Interglacial soils frequently have complex profiles, suggesting they were developed under a sequence of vegetational types. Finally, she points out that these soils are very thick-- the total depth of weathering often amounts to as much as 4-5 m, indicating that the Last Interglacial was a very pronounced warm interval, perhaps at its height warmer than the present. The fact that the level of the Black Sea, the Karangat

Sea of the Last Interglacial (see map 4), was higher than at present also suggests very warm conditions by implying that less water was locked up in the planetary ice caps.

Early Würm Environments

Pollen data from the initial phase of the Last Glacial are very sparse in the European USSR. Perhaps the best information comes from deposits that overlie the cultural horizon at Khotylevo. These deposits contain pollen of dwarf birch (*Betula nana*) and other plants that as a group are characteristic today of northern Finland (Grichuk 1969a:46). This suggests that the opening phase of the Last Glacial was quite cold indeed.

Following its very cold beginning, the early Würm was interrupted by a complex interval of milder climate known in the European USSR as the Upper Volga Interstadial (Amersfoort or Broerup Interstadials or both of Northern Europe-- see fig. 1). A pollen diagram from the locality of Turchinka (see map 4) in the Pripyat' Basin has supplied the clearest picture of Upper Volga vegetation in the region north of Kiev. This diagram is reproduced here in figure 4 (top). Basically, it implies climatic conditions similar to, though somewhat cooler and drier than, those of the end of the Last Interglacial (Grichuk 1969a:46-47; 1969c:452-53). It suggests forest-steppe vegetation, with pine and birch predominant in the forests; for the most part, pollen of oak, elm, linden, and so forth, is so infrequent that it may have been blown in from far distant areas. These trees, therefore, may not have occurred locally.

Pollen data from the Carpathians suggest that, at the beginning of the Würm, the major vegetation belts there were depressed at least 1000 m while even during the Upper Volga Interstadial, depression on the order of 600 m occurred (Grichuk 1969a:49). This could account for the discovery of charcoal of fir (*Abies alba*) in horizon 11 of Molodova V on the middle Dnestr (Ivanova and Chernysh 1965:199). It was pointed out in chapter 2 that this horizon, along with horizons 12A and 12 of the same site and Mousterian levels 1-5 of Molodova I, clearly date from the early Würm and perhaps from the Upper Volga Interstadial. Fir is not present in the vicinity of Molodova today; its nearest occurrence is

42

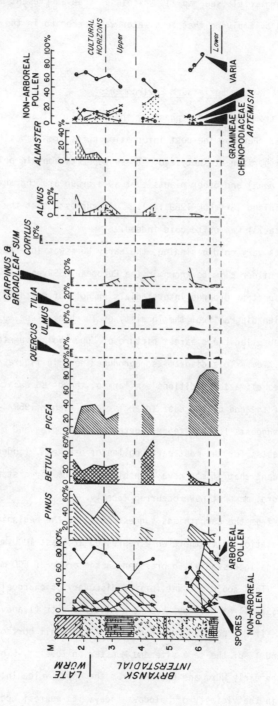

Fig. 5A.--Kostenki XVII. Pollen diagram.

43

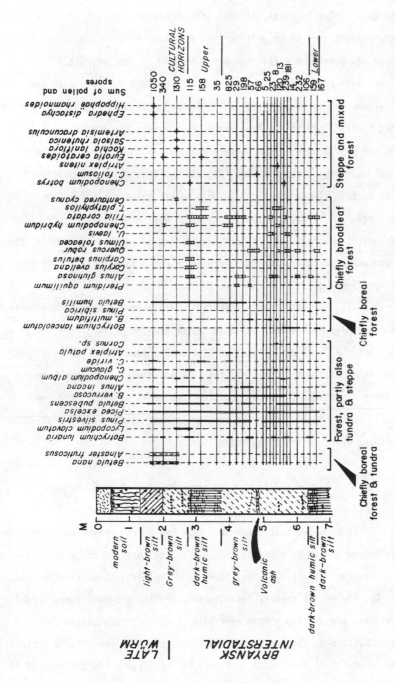

Fig. 5B.--Kostenki XVII. Floral diagram. (Figs. 5A and 5B based on analyses by V. P. Grichuk; redrawn after Grichuk 1969b, figs. 16 and 17.)

on the high slopes of the Carpathians to the southwest.

The Upper Volga Interstadial was succeeded by an interval of intense cold, at the beginning of which gelifluction and other frost processes contorted and otherwise disrupted the soils that had developed in the interstadial. Although loess-like deposits dating from the post-Upper Volga cold snap are fairly well-known in European Russia, investigators have only recently succeeded in obtaining identifiable pollen from them. Pollen data now available from deposits in the middle Dnepr basin suggest that it was characterized by an extremely cold and dry steppe (Grichuk 1969c:454). Tree pollen comprises no more than 12 percent of the total and belongs mainly to shrub-like birches (*Betula nana* and *B. humilis*) and the cold-loving dwarf alder (*Alnaster fruti-cosus*). Today this plant is only found several hundred kilometers north of the middle Dnepr, where it usually grows on ground in which the substratum is permanently frozen (permafrost).

No archeological sites that undoubtedly date from the time of the early Würm maximum cold have so far been found in the Ukraine or nearby regions. It is conceivable that the level of cultural development achieved in Europe at the time was insufficient to allow occupation of the area under what must have been extremely harsh conditions. However, several more years of systematic reconnaissance will be necessary before the possibility may be discounted that sites of the right age exist but remain unfound.

Middle Würm Environments

It will be recalled that the middle Würm was a long period of fluctuating climate, following the early Würm cold maximum. Data to reconstruct the environment of the European USSR are only available from the terminal part of the middle Wurm, known locally as the Bryansk Interstadial. Pollen diagrams characterizing this interstadial are available from several localities in the central part of the European USSR. A particularly informative diagram from the site of Kostenki XVII on the Don River is reproduced in figure 5A. In figure 5B, the data of 5A are rearranged so as to make clear the outstanding features of the diagram.

Fundamentally, the available pollen data indicate that conditions were considerably milder than during the cold maxima of the Last Glacial. Forest-steppe was the rule in the central part of the European USSR, while the forests contained a mixture of elements (spruce, hornbeam, linden, and so forth) which indicate that the climate was neither very cold nor very warm. At Molodova on the Dnestr, conifers presently unknown in the area grew alongside oak, which is the predominant tree there today (pine charcoal was found at Molodova V in horizons 7, 8, and 10; spruce charcoal in horizon 9; and oak charcoal in horizon 8 [Ivanova and Chernysh 1965:199]).

Fairly deep soils with weathering profiles up to 1½ m thick developed during the Bryansk Interstadial. For the most part, they suggest forest-steppe conditions, with emphasis on the steppe (Morozova 1969b, 1969c). In detail, they are unlike any of the soils that developed in the European USSR during the Last Interglacial or Holocene, presumably because of the unusual mix of vegetation that grew on them. Repeated and extended intervals of severe frost may also have played a role in producing the peculiar appearance of Bryansk soils.

Late Würm Environments

The Bryansk Interstadial was followed by a return to very cold conditions. This is clearly indicated by frost disturbance of the Bryansk soils in a number of localities (Velichko 1969b) and even more clearly by pollen data such as those collected at Kostenki XVII (figs. 5A and 5B). Broad-leaf trees disappeared from most areas they had previously grown in, and such cold-loving plants as dwarf birch and dwarf alder took their place. So, for example, charcoal of birch has been found at the middle Desna site of Chulatovo II, occupied at the very end of the Bryansk Interstadial or the very beginning of the late Würm (Boriskovskij 1953:290). Pollen and sedimentological-geomorphological data indicate that except for a minor break around 17,000-16,000 B.P., extreme cold characterized the late Würm until glacial conditions generally began to wane, about 13,000 or 14,000 B.P. Ice-wedge casts and other frost structures suggest that during this interval permafrost reached as far south as latitudes 47°-48°N (see map 5), while nearly permanently frozen ground, characterized by only a very brief interval of

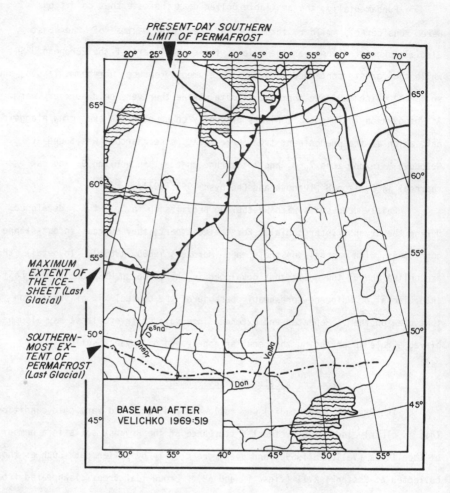

Map 5.--Distribution of permafrost today and in the Last Glacial. (After Velichko 1969b:519.)

complete thawing, stretched to the Black Sea (Velichko 1969b:436). Grichuk

(1969b:65) has estimated that average January temperatures in the Ukraine and

nearby regions were lowered by as much as 8° or 9°C (14-16°F).

Sufficient pollen data are available to construct a hypothetical vegeta-

tion map for the European USSR during the time of maximum cold of the Late Würm.

One such map, recently compiled by Grichuk (1969c), is reproduced here as map 6.

It shows that the Ukraine and nearby regions would have been covered primarily

by a kind of steppe with plants indicating very cold, dry conditions. This

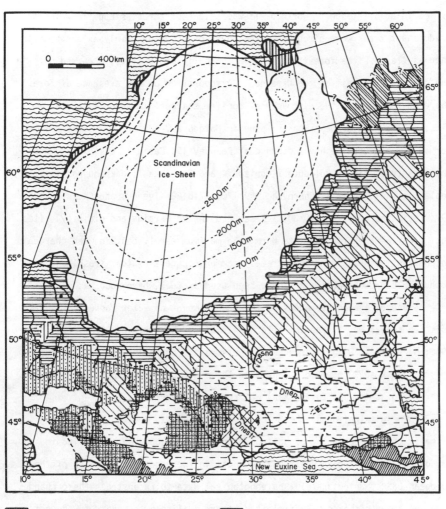

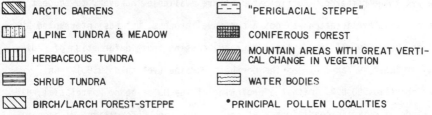

ARCTIC BARRENS		"PERIGLACIAL STEPPE"	
ALPINE TUNDRA & MEADOW		CONIFEROUS FOREST	
HERBACEOUS TUNDRA		MOUNTAIN AREAS WITH GREAT VERTICAL CHANGE IN VEGETATION	
SHRUB TUNDRA		WATER BODIES	
BIRCH/LARCH FOREST-STEPPE		•PRINCIPAL POLLEN LOCALITIES	
BROADLEAF FOREST-STEPPE			

Map 6.--Vegetation zones of central and eastern Europe during the late Würm cold maximum. (After Grichuk 1969c:626.)

steppe, having no precise modern counterparts, is known to Soviet investigators as "periglacial steppe." North of it was a zone of forest-steppe in which the predominant trees were birch and larch, perhaps occuring mainly as shrubs rather than as trees. True forest, composed principally of conifers, occurred only in the extreme southwest of the Ukraine. Corroboration of the presence of forest there may be seen in the discovery of conifer charcoal in several late Würm sites in the middle Dnestr basin: pine in Molodova V-horizon 6, Oselivka I, Korman II, and Chutuleshty I; spruce at Rozhnev II, Babin I, Lisichniki, and Chutuleshty I; fir in Molodova I-horizon 4 and Oselivka I; oak and possibly poplar at Chutuleshty I (Chernysh 1959:170; 171b:68; Ivanova and Chernysh 1965: 199; David and Ketraru 1970:30). Elsewhere in the Ukraine and vicinity, sites that clearly date from the late Würm cold maximum rarely contain wood charcoal. In contrast, charred bone is extremely common, suggesting that fresh bone with combustible organic matter may have been used as fuel where wood was scarce.

One of the consequences of the great amount of water locked up in late Würm ice sheets was a drop in world sea level on the order of 130 m (Guilcher 1969; Bloom 1971, with references). The straits separating the Mediterranean and the Black seas became dry land, and the Black Sea (see map 6, where it is referred to as the New Euxine Sea) was considerably reduced in extent.

The dissipation of the Scandinavian ice sheet, and the accompanying climatic change, beginning probably around 14,000-13,000 years ago, led to pronounced shifts and compositional changes in the vegetational belts of the European USSR. Unfortunately, paleobotanical data to reconstruct these changes have yet to be gathered. Sufficient data are available, however, to suggest that climatic amelioration was not a continual process, but was interrupted by periods when very cold conditions returned, causing frost deformation of sediments at least as far south as the northern Ukraine (Velichko 1969b). Only after about 10,000 B.P., with the beginning of the Holocene or Postglacial, did the kinds of climatic conditions that could cause such deformations disappear for good.

The extraordinary cold that characterized the European USSR during most of the late Würm was obviously no barrier to human occupation, as numerous

archeological sites show. These sites contain a variety of evidence to suggest
that the late Würm inhabitants of the region were well adapted to the harsh
environment in which they lived. In fact, the late Würm occupants of the Ukraine
and nearby areas probably achieved higher population densities than either their
predecessors in the middle Würm or their successors in the early Holocene. These
relatively high population densities were made possible by the remarkable richness of game on the "periglacial steppe," in combination with the relatively
well-developed hunting capabilities of late Würm peoples. At first thought, it
may seem strange that an environment like the periglacial steppe could support
an extremely rich and varied mammilian fauna, but in fact, theoretical considerations, as well as empirical evidence from archeological sites, indicate this was
the case. Even during times of maximum cold, summers were probably warm enough
to encourage a fairly rich growth of edible fodder. And although the winters
were undoubtedly very long and very cold, they were relatively dry, so that the
past summer's growth was not buried beneath a deep snowcover.

Faunal Remains from Early Man Sites and Their Implications

Faunal remains found in occupation sites constitute the best source of
information on the way in which early man in the Ukraine and elsewhere interacted
with his environment. Species lists have now been published for most of the
important sites, and in many instances information is also available on species
frequencies. Sometimes this frequency information is restricted to relative
terms like "few," "some," or "many" appended to a species name; but in many
cases, there are estimates of the minimum numbers of individuals by which each
species is represented at a site. Most commonly, these estimates are based on
counts of one-to-an-animal skeletal parts--the largest number of such parts for
any given species equaling the minimum number of individuals by which that
species is represented.

The geographic and temporal distribution of various species in the
Ukraine and nearby areas is shown in table 4. The minimum number of individuals
by which each species is represented, as well as the number of sites it occurs

TABLE 4

PRINCIPAL MAMMALIAN SPECIES REPRESENTED IN EARLY MAN SITES IN THE UKRAINE AND NEARBY AREAS, GROUPED BY AREA AND TIME INTERVAL

Species	Eem (Mous.) Dnepr-Desna	Early Würm (Mous.) Dnestr	Early Würm (Mous.) Dnepr-Desna	Middle Würm (Mous.) Dnestr	Middle Würm (Mous.) Dnepr-Desna	Middle Würm (Upper Paleo.) Dnestr	Middle Würm (Upper Paleo.) Dnepr-Desna	Late Würm (Upper Paleo.) Dnestr	Late Würm (Upper Paleo.) Dnepr-Desna	Late Würm (Upper Paleo.) Other	Present Status in Ukraine and Vicinity (Based on information in Burton 1962; Bobrinskij et al. 1965; and Kurten 1968)	Preferred Habitat
Mammuthus primigenius, woolly mammoth	x	xx	x	x		x	xx	x	xx	x	Totally extinct	Open country, middle and upper latitudes
Coelodonta antiquitatis, woolly rhinoceros		x	x	x		x		x	x	+	Totally extinct	Open country, middle and upper latitudes
Equus caballus, wild horse	x	x		x		xx	x	xx	x	x	Extinct in Ukraine	Open country, middle latitudes
Bison priscus, steppe bison	?			x		x		x	x	xx	Totally extinct	Open country, middle latitudes
Bos primigenius, aurochs	?					+		+		x	Totally extinct	Open woodlands, middle latitudes
Capra or *Ovis*, wild sheep or goat								+			Extinct in Ukraine	Open country with high relief
Ovibus moschatus, musk-ox									+		Extinct in Ukraine	Open country, upper latitudes
Saiga tatarica, saiga antelope									+		Extinct in Ukraine	Open country, middle latitudes
Rangifer tarandus, reindeer	x		x	x		xx	x	xx	x	x	Extinct in Ukraine	Open country and woodland, upper latitudes
Cervus elaphus, red deer	x		x	x		x	x	x	x		---	Open country and woodland, middle latitudes
Capreolus capreolus, roe deer								+			---	Woodlands, middle latitudes
Alces alces, moose						+		+			---	Woodlands, upper latitudes

Species							Status	Habitat
Megaloceros giganteus, giant deer					×	×	Totally extinct	Open woodlands, middle latitudes
Canis lupus, wolf	×	×	×	×	×	×	--	Various zones, various latitudes
Vulpes vulpes, ordinary red fox	×	+	+	×	+	×	--	Various zones, various latitudes
Alopex lagopus, arctic fox	×	×		xx	×		Extinct in Ukraine	Open country, upper latitudes
Ursus arctos, brown bear	×	×	×	×		×	--	Forests, middle latitudes
Crocuta spelaea, cave hyena							Totally extinct	Various zones, middle and lower latitudes
Felis leo spelaea, cave lion		+	+			+	Totally extinct	Various zones, various latitudes
Lynx lynx, lynx	×	+	+			+	--	Forests, middle and upper latitudes
Meles meles, badger	×	+	+	×	×	×	--	Woodland, middle latitudes
Gulo gulo, wolverine	×	×	×	×	×	×	--	Forests, upper latitudes
Marmota bobac, steppe marmot	×	×	×	×	×	×	Extinct in Ukraine	Open country, middle latitudes
Lepus sp., hare	+	+	×	×	×	×	--	Various zones, various latitudes
Aves, birds								
Pisces, fish								

+ = rare occurrence; × = common occurrence; ×× = very common occurrence

Sources:

For Dnestr sites: Ambrozewicz (1930); Boriskovskij (1953); Botez (1933); Chernysh (1959, 1965, 1968a, 1968b, 1969, 1970); David and Ketraru (1970); Ivanova (1962, 1968); Ivanova and Chernysh (1965).

For Dnepr-Desna sites: Boriskovskij (1953); Boriskovskij and Praslov (1964); Grishchenko (1971); Gromov (1948); Gvozdover (1958); Mesyats (1957); Pidoplichko (1969); Polikarpovich (1968); Savich (1968, 1969a, 1969b); Shovkoplyas (1965a, 1965b, 1967); Zavernyaev (1970).

For other sites: Boriskovskij (1953); Boriskovskij and Praslov (1964); Chernysh (1953); Petrichenko (1961, 1963).

in for each area-time interval, has been used to provide a rough guide of
relative species abundance, as expressed in the table. It is important to
realize that the table masks frequency variation among sites within a region
(for example, not all late Würm sites in the Dnepr-Desna basin contain more
mammoth than reindeer, though most do). It is also important to understand the
limitations placed on the interpretation of table 4 by the fact that not all time
intervals are equally rich in sites. As was pointed out in the conclusions to
chapter 2 (see also table 2), the late Würm is far richer than earlier periods.
It is quite possible that the principal differences between the species lists
of the late Würm and of the earlier periods are due simply to chance ("sampling
error"). Differences in site density are less likely to lead to chance differences in species lists when comparison involves lists from different regions in
the same time interval. This is especially true for the comparison of regions
in the late Würm. Reasonably large numbers of sites are known from both major
geographic regions (Dnestr and Dnepr-Desna) for that interval.

Examination of the last column of table 4 shows that most of the species,
including all those represented in quantity, prefer open (as opposed to forested)
landscapes. This is in accord with previously cited pollen data indicating that
the Ukraine and neighboring regions were characterized primarily by steppe or
forest-steppe from the terminal part of the Last Interglacial (when human occupation is first securely documented) throughout the Last Glacial. From table 4
it is also apparent that most of the species represented are herbivores, while,
among these, animals which are believed to have lived in herds (mammoth, horse,
bison, and reindeer) have been found in the greatest frequency.

Mammoth bones are the hallmark of Ukrainian early man sites, occurring
in all but a very few, for example, Amvrosievka, Bol'shaya Akkarzha, Rogalik,
and Zhuravka, which in fact may date from the very late Würm or even the early
Holocene, when mammoth had become extinct. In many cases it was the discovery
of mammoth bones--which are hard to miss--that led to the discovery of a site.
Not one of the sites where mammoth bones have been found, however, clearly
represents a place where they were killed. In fact, it is now known that in
virtually every site in which mammoth is especially common (the early Würm sites

of Molodova I and V on the Dnestr and the late Würm or late middle Würm sites of Berdyzh, Dobranichevka, Eliseevichi, Gontsy, Kirillovskaya, Mezhirich, Mezin, Pushkari I, Radomyshl', and Yudinovo in the Dnepr-Desna basin)[2] the overwhelming majority of mammoth bones occurred in patterned arrangements suggesting ruins (see chap. 4). The individual bones seem to have served as constructional material and were probably brought to the sites specifically for this purpose. This is strongly implied by the fact that some parts of the skeleton--especially scapulae, pelves, certain long bones, mandibles, and skulls--are disproportionately represented. It is further implied by the enormous effort that concentrating the bones at the sites must have involved. A defleshed and dried mammoth skull with relatively small tusks weighed a minimum of 100 kg (220 lbs.) (Vereshchagin 1967:380), and other large bones were far from light.

It has generally been assumed that the mammoth bones found in Ukrainian sites were obtained almost entirely from animals killed in the hunt, though the difficulties in killing such large beasts on a regular basis must have been very great. In fact, given the extensive use of mammoth bone in construction, the possibility must be considered that many, if not most, of the bones were scavenged from the skeletons of animals that had died naturally. This is especially suggested for the sites of Mezin and Mezhirich, where systematic examination of the mammoth bones has shown that many were gnawed by carnivores (Shovkoplyas 1965b; Pidoplichko 1969:115). In addition, chemical analyses of the bones from Mezin indicate that mammoths of very much different geologic antiquity may be represented in a single mammoth bone "ruin."

Besides being used in construction, "naturally" occurring mammoth bones may also have been collected for fuel. Small bits of charred bone are especially common in late Würm sites of the Dnepr-Desna basin, for which paleobotanical data suggest that trees would have been relatively rare. In this context, it is

---

2. The minimum numbers of mammoths represented in the Dnepr-Desna sites were: Berdyzh 45 (Gromov 1948:159; Polikarpovich 1968:29), Dobranichevka 28 (Pidoplichko 1969:51), Kirillovskaya 70 (Boriskovskij and Praslov 1964:32), Mezhirich 95 (Pidoplichko 1969:115), Mezin 116 (Shovkoplyas 1965b:97), Pushkari I 65 (Boriskovskij 1953:226), Radomyshl' 47 (Shovkoplyas 1965a), and Yudinovo 50 (Polikarpovich 1968:167).

interesting that mammoth bones are comparatively infrequent in late Würm sites on the Dnestr, where trees were apparently more abundant (chap. 2). The relative abundance of trees on the Dnestr, of course, also meant that wood would have been more readily available for the construction of shelters.

After mammoth, reindeer and horse are the most frequently found animals in the late Würm Dnepr-Desna sites, while they are always more common than mammoth in late Würm sites on the Dnestr. This contrast between the Dnepr-Desna and the Dnestr in the late Würm may reflect paleoenvironmental differences if it can be assumed that the large accumulations of mammoth bones found at Dnepr-Desna sites in one way or another reflect the scarcity of trees there. Additional evidence that trees were less common in the Dnepr-Desna drainage may be seen in the absence there of roe deer, red deer, and moose. Remains of these predominantly woodland creatures have been found in some late Würm sites on the Dnestr, though admittedly in small numbers. A final suggestion of environmental differences between the Dnepr-Desna and the Dnestr drainages in the late Würm is the presence of wild sheep or goats at some Dnestr sites. These creatures presumably were taken in the nearby foothills of the Carpathians, where suitable habitats for them probably existed.

Most of the horse and reindeer bones found in early man sites in the Ukraine and nearby areas were fractured in such a way as to suggest that the marrow was extracted. This in turn suggests that these animals were systematically hunted for food. It is possible that at some sites a portion of the reindeer remains, especially the antlers, were scavenged, since they were used to manufacture artifacts and build shelters,[3] but in most cases it seems reasonable to suppose that the reindeer were killed by the human occupants.

If, by analogy with modern reindeer, it may be assumed that Last Glacial reindeer gave birth primarily in late spring or early summer, analysis of reindeer bones may provide information on the season of the year that a site was occupied. Such analyses have been made of reindeer remains from Mezin

---

3. Reindeer antlers that seem to have been used in construction have been found in Molodova V-horizon 2 (Chernysh 1959:102-3) and Mezin (Shovkoplyas 1965b:97). At Mezin, many of the antlers representing a minimum of 83 individuals appear to have been naturally shed.

(Shovkoplyas 1965b:97ff) and Dobranichevka (Pidoplichko 1969:67). Neither site turned out to contain remains of newborn or very young animals, strongly suggesting that neither was occupied in summer. As will be pointed out below, corroborating evidence that these sites and others were not occupied in the warmer months may be seen in the scarcity or total absence of remains of game birds and fish. Given the behavior of modern reindeer and the sharp contrast that existed between summer and winter during the Last Glacial in the Ukraine, it is almost certain that the reindeer (and probably other major grazing mammals) were migratory. In the summer months, the herds, and with them the people of Mezin and Dobranichevka, may have been farther to the north.

As a final point on reindeer, it is important to note that their occurrence in early man sites is of course indicative of very cold conditions. There is no record of reindeer penetrating into the Ukraine in the Holocene. Cold conditions are perhaps even more strongly implied for some sites by the presence of musk-oxen, restricted to the North American and Greenland tundra today.[4]

Among the remaining herbivores, the only one that is commonly represented at early man sites is the steppe bison. It occurs more or less consistently at late Würm sites in both the Dnestr and Dnepr-Desna basins, but is only really abundant at the localities of Bol'shaya Akkarzha and Amvrosievka in the far south of the Ukraine (map 2). At Amvrosievka, several hundred individuals are represented (Boriskovskij and Praslov 1964:23). The geologic antiquity of these two sites is not entirely clear, but if it may be assumed that they are roughly contemporaneous with sites on the Dnestr, where horse and reindeer predominate, and with sites in the Dnepr-Desna drainage, where mammoth is most abundant, then their extraordinary content of bison may constitute additional evidence for paleoenvironmental variation in the late Würm of the Ukraine.

Carnivore remains are generally rare in early man sites (see, for example, Klein 1971:147 and 1972), and the Ukraine constitutes no exception. The scarcity

---

4. Musk-ox has been reported from Dobranichevka (Pidoplichko 1969:67), Mezin (where 17 individuals are said to be represented [Shovkoplyas 1965b:97]), and Bugorok (Boriskovskij 1953:235).

of carnivore bones presumably reflects both the relative rarity of carnivores in the ancient environment, and the difficulty of hunting them, especially the more dangerous ones like the lion and the bear. Among the carnivores represented in Ukrainian sites, only arctic fox and wolf occur in any frequency.[5] Both seem to have been hunted largely for their pelts. The evidence for this assertion is the repeated discovery--for example, at Mezin (Shovkoplyas 1965b) and Avdeevo (Rogachev 1953)--of whole or nearly whole skeletons of these animals, possessing everything but the paws, presumably removed with the skins. Correspondingly, articulated paw skeletons have been found separately. Something about the hunting habits of the people of Eliseevichi--probably their desire for mature pelts--is reflected in the age distribution of the arctic foxes they killed. The site contained remains belonging to 6 foxes less than 8 months old, 16 in the vicinity of 1 year, 13 in the vicinity of 2 years, and 5 aged about 3 years (Polikarpovich 1968). The age distribution in a modern free-ranging population of the same size would most likely be 20 individuals under 8 months, 7 aged about 1 year, 7 aged about 2 years, and 3 aged about 3 years. At some sites (for example, Gontsy [Pidoplichko 1969:51]), in addition to wolves or arctic foxes, hares may have been utilized for pelts. This is suggested both by their abundance (no less than 16 individuals at Gontsy) and by the discovery of detached but articulated hare paws.

The only rodent that was probably large enough to attract the systematic attention of early man in the Ukraine was the steppe marmot. Its disarticulated remains, indicating that it was indeed hunted, have been found at several sites. Remains of other rodents have been found at most sites, but generally in conditions that suggest the animals died in their burrows, that is, their remains usually occur as complete skeletons. It is certainly relevant to point out that many burrowing rodents prefer disturbed ground and may have congregated at early man sites after (or even before) they were abandoned. Even though most rodents occur as "natural" intrusions in sites, they are not without interest. The

---

5. Domestic dogs have been reported from Mezin (Shovkoplyas 1965a:97) and Eliseevichi (Polikarpovich 1968:50), but these claims have not yet received detailed substantiation. As elsewhere, the domestic dog is not clearly present in the European USSR until the early Holocene.

discovery of the collared or snow lemming (*Dicrostonyx torquatus*) in early Würm

sites on the Dnestr (Molodova I and V) and in late Würm sites in the Dnepr-Desna

drainage (Chulatovo I, Mezin, Novogorod-Severskij, and Pushkari I) is especially

interesting, since this creature is an unquestionable indicator of colder condi-

tions than prevail in the Ukraine at present. Perhaps even more interesting is

the fact that the snow lemming is found in the same sites as such typically

steppe rodents as the great jerboa (*Allactaga jaculus*). The ranges of these two

rodents come nowhere near overlapping today. Their co-occurrence in late Würm

sites serves to support the notion, based on paleobotanical data, that the

periglacial steppe was an environment without modern counterparts.[6]

Creatures other than mammals are remarkably scarce in early man sites in

the Ukraine and vicinity. Remains of crows (*Corvus corax*) and owls (*Bubo bubo*,

Strix uralensis, and *Nyctea scandiaca*) have been reported from several sites,

but in very small numbers. They probably derive from animals that died naturally;

the owls in particular may represent creatures which nested in the ruins of

structures. Only the snowy owl (*N. scandiaca*) found at Mezin (Shovkoplyas 1965b:

97) deserves special note, since it is yet another indicator of very cold climate

(Flint, V. E., et al. 1968:350-51).

Remains of game birds are very rare in Ukrainian sites. The only one

found in any frequency is the cold-loving willow ptarmigan or snowy partridge

(*Lagopus lagopus*), known from a small quantity of bones at Avdeevo, Dobranichevka,

Eliseevichi, Mezhirich, and Mezin. Waterfowl are represented by bones or

eggshell fragments only at Mezin (Shovkoplyas 1965b:97) and Avdeevo (Gvozdover

1958:13). Their rarity at these sites and their total absence elsewhere may be

interpreted as evidence that the sites were occupied primarily in winter, when

migratory birds would have been far to the south. The near absence of fish

remains, reported only from Eliseevichi (Polikarpovich 1968:50) and Chulatovo I

(Boriskovskij 1953:300), and then only in very small quantities, may also reflect

---

6. Similar evidence of uniqueness exists for the periglacial steppe of
Siberia (Klein 1971:142) and of central Europe (Butzer 1967; Frenzel 1964;
Kowalski 1967:354).

the fact that the sites were inhabited primarily in winter, when fishing in the frozen rivers would have been impractical.

It is in fact possible that virtually all the known sites represent winter camps built in the comparative shelter of the river valleys. Summer encampments may have been located primarily on the interfluves, where the herds of horse, reindeer, bison, and mammoth grazed. The relative lack of exposures through Last Glacial deposits on the interfluves makes it difficult to find sites there. Summer encampments may also have been comparatively transitory, leaving behind less debris to catch the archeologist's eye.

Megafaunal Extinctions in the Ukraine

As elsewhere in middle latitude Europe, near the end of the Last Glacial, several large mammals became extinct in the Ukraine. These were the woolly mammoth, woolly rhinoceros, steppe bison, giant deer, reindeer, musk-ox, arctic fox, lion, and hyena.[7] The disappearance of the lion and hyena, if indeed they disappeared (there is some evidence that at least the lion survived), may be attributed to the disappearance of the other animals, at least some of which they relied upon for food. The steppe bison may have become "extinct" by evolving into the forest bison (*Bison bonasus*) of the European Holocene (Kowalski 1967: 357), while the reindeer and arctic fox were probably simply displaced northwards as a result of environmental change. Both survived to the present in the northern parts of the European USSR. It might have been supposed a priori that the musk-ox would simply have retreated north as well, but if it did, it has so far escaped detection in Eurasian Holocene deposits. It seems to have survived only in the North American and Greenland tundra.

The most puzzling terminal Pleistocene extinctions are those of the mammoth, rhinoceros, and giant deer (a giant more in antler than in body size). Although it is probable that they did not become extinct everywhere simultaneously, not one of the three seems to have survived the Pleistocene anywhere

---

7. Wild horse, aurochs, saiga antelope, and steppe marmot, also listed as "extinct in the Ukraine" in table 4, are victims of historic man.

in Eurasia. Some authors (for example, Kowalski 1967, Vereshchagin 1967, Reed 1970) believe that environmental change (especially the expansion of forests) must have been the major reason. Others, above all Martin (1967), argue that man played the major role. However, Martin's case rests mainly on data from North America, where terminal Pleistocene-early Holocene extinctions were far more extensive and may have occurred only shortly after man first appeared on the scene.

The problem is far from being resolved. If environmental change is the answer, it seems strange that the woolly rhino and the woolly mammoth both survived the comparable change at the end of the Penultimate Glacial. If man played a major role, it is curious that it was the mammoth and rhino that disappeared rather than the aurochs, red deer, and wild horse, which were probably hunted much more intensively. It is probable that causation here was complex. For example, it is possible that environmental stress placed on mammoth and rhino populations at the end of the Last Glacial reduced their numbers to the point where human activities could provide the coup de grâce. Similar stress may have acted on mammoth and rhino populations at the end of the Penultimate Glacial but the men of that time may have been culturally incapable of delivering the final blow or even of following relict populations into refugia that probably included parts of the European USSR.

Whatever solution to the extinctions problem is finally accepted, it may someday prove relevant that the woolly rhinoceros and the steppe bison may have survived the mammoth in the Ukraine by a millenium or two. This is suggested at several sites, especially at Molodova V, where mammoth is last recorded in horizon 3 with a date of 13,370 ± 540, while the rhino and steppe bison persist in levels 1A and 1 respectively, dated to between 11,000 and 10,000 B.P. (table 2).

Conclusions

The very presence of fairly numerous archeological sites shows that the rather harsh environments of the Last Glacial and especially of the late Würm were far from lifeless. The abundance of animal remains in these sites indicates clearly that human beings survived, and perhaps even thrived through the exploitation of relatively varied and reasonably abundant game. In addition, since virtually all historically known peoples to whom hunting was a major form of subsistence also utilized plants to a greater or lesser extent (some Eskimoes being the major exceptions), it is possible to suppose that the Last Glacial inhabitants of the Ukraine did so as well. Unfortunately, this is difficult to document since plant refuse does not fossilize as readily as bones do. It is now known, however, that tiny charred seeds, which may escape the eye of the excavator, can turn up in sizeable numbers if special techniques are used to find them (Struever 1968). The application of such techniques to sediment samples from Ukrainian sites may one day give us a better idea of the extent to which Last Glacial peoples there utilized plants.

Animal remains are not the only evidence of human adaptations to Last Glacial environments in the Ukraine. There are also numerous and often spectacular cultural debris (artifacts and "features") found in occupation sites. These, and the technological ingenuity they imply, are the subject of the next chapter.

4. CULTURAL REMAINS

Last Interglacial Sites

Only Khotylevo on the Desna has provided a large artifact assemblage that is clearly of Last Interglacial age. Unmodified flakes and blades predominate among the 90,000 flint artifacts found at this site, but there are also several thousand pieces with systematic edge modification or retouch (Zavernyaev 1961, 1971; Zavernyaev and Schmidt 1961). These retouched pieces have not been described in detail; but it is clear that they belong to the same stone-tool types that characterize the early Würm and early middle Würm sites of the Ukraine.

Artifacts from Early Würm and Early Middle Würm Sites

The artifact assemblages from the early Würm and early middle Wurm sites share a number of important features. The bulk of each assemblage consists of unretouched flakes, made of flint that was obtained nearby. Each assemblage also contains a variable number of unretouched blades (flakes that are at least twice as long as wide), debris (formless flint hunks), and cores. As might be expected, the cores belong principally to types from which flakes, rather than blades, were struck. Disc-shaped (or discoid) cores, from which flakes were removed radially on one or both surfaces (fig. 6, nos. 1, 2), are especially common. Occasionally, cores have been found on which the surface was specially prepared beforehand to allow removal of a flake of predetermined size and shape.

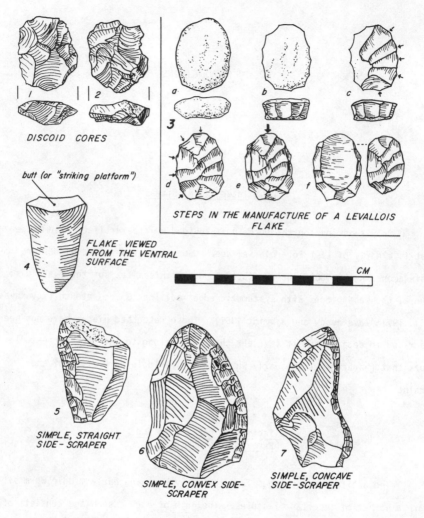

DISCOID CORES

butt (or "striking platform")

FLAKE VIEWED
FROM THE VENTRAL
SURFACE

STEPS IN THE MANUFACTURE OF A LEVALLOIS
FLAKE

CM

SIMPLE, STRAIGHT
SIDE-SCRAPER

SIMPLE, CONVEX SIDE-
SCRAPER

SIMPLE, CONCAVE
SIDE-SCRAPER

Fig. 6.--Mousterian stone artifacts I. (Nos. 1, 2 after Chernysh 1959, fig. 26; 3 after Bordes 1961b, fig. 4; 4-7 after Bordes 1961a, fig. 1, pls. 14, 17.)

Such cores and the flakes they were designed to produce are referred to as *Levallois*. (See fig. 6, no. 3, for an explanation of the manufacture of a Levallois flake.) They are generally uncommon in the Ukraine, although the number varies somewhat from site to site.

In addition to cores and unretouched flakes, blades, and debris, each of the Ukrainian assemblages also contains a small proportion of retouched pieces.

Most common among these are flakes on which one or more edges has been retouched to form tools known as *side-scrapers*. (The name is misleading, since it is far from certain that all or even most side-scrapers were used for scraping, as opposed, say, to cutting.) Following the typological scheme set forth by Bordes (1961a), several types of side-scrapers have been recognized from Ukrainian sites (Klein 1969a, 1970; Anisyutkin 1969). The principal differentiating criteria are the shape of the retouched edge, the number of retouched edges, and the position of the edge(s) relative to the *butt* of the flake, that is, the part of the flake which received the blow when the core was struck. (The butt is sometimes known as the "striking platform.") (See fig. 6, no. 4.) So, for example, a flake on which a single edge, lying more or less perpendicular to the butt, has been re-touched is known as a *simple side-scraper*. It can be simple straight (fig. 6, no. 5), simple convex (fig. 6, no. 6), or simple concave (fig. 6, no. 7). The edge that is retouched may also be the one opposite (parallel or subparallel to) the butt, in which case the side-scraper is said to be *transverse*. Again, dif-ferent types of transverse side-scrapers may be defined by the shape of the retouched edge (fig. 7, nos. 1, 2, 3).

Flakes occur on which two parallel or subparallel edges, both more or less perpendicular to the butt, have been retouched. These are known as *double side-scrapers* (fig. 7, nos. 4-6). Examples are also common on which two retouched edges converge to a point. If the point is relatively sharp and the flake itself is relatively thin, such an artifact may actually be called a *point*. However, if the point is dull or the flake is fairly thick (so that it would be hard to imagine using it as a point), the retouched piece is known as a *convergent side-scraper* (fig. 7, no. 7). A special kind of convergent side-scraper, known as a *canted* (or *dejété*) *side-scraper*, is formed when one of two converging retouched edges lies parallel or near-parallel (transverse) to the butt of the flake (fig. 7, no. 8). Different varieties of double, convergent, and canted side-scrapers can obviously be defined by combinations of edges of different shapes. In practice, two or more combinations are often lumped as a single type because each combination may be represented only by a small number of specimens at a given site.

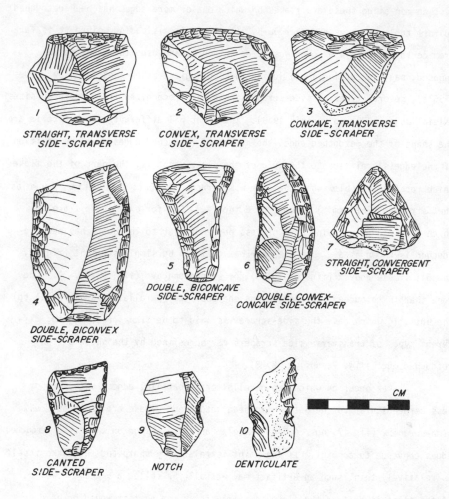

Fig. 7.--Mousterian stone artifacts II. (After Bordes 1961a, pls. 18, 19, 22, 39, 40.)

Most often, the retouch that forms a side-scraper is located on the surface of the flake that was on the outside of the core before the flake was struck. This surface is known as the *dorsal surface* and is generally rougher than the opposite or *ventral surface*. (The roughness is a result of the ridges surrounding negative scars left behind by the removal of prior flakes from the core.) Sometimes, however, the side-scraper retouch is located on the ventral surface, in which case a special kind of side-scraper ("*on ventral surface*") may be recognized. Other peculiarities, such as retouch on both the dorsal and ventral surfaces (bifacial retouch) or retouch that is extremely abrupt (dulling) may also be used to define special side-scraper types. The various special types are comparatively rare, especially in the Ukraine.

After side-scrapers, the most frequently found retouched tools in Ukrainian early and early middle Würm sites are *notches*, *denticulates*, and pieces which probably received their retouch in the process of utilization. ("Utilization retouch" is usually very fine, abrupt, and discontinuous.) A notch is simply a flake on whose edge a distinct hollow has been deliberately formed   (fig. 7, no. 9). A denticulate is a flake with several contiguous notches (fig. 7, no. 10). Some sites also contain small numbers of other recognizable tool types, particularly such things as end-scrapers and burins which are extremely common in late middle Würm and late Würm sites and which will be discussed in greater detail below. It is important to point out here that the end-scrapers and burins which have been found in early and early middle Würm sites in the Ukraine are not only rare, they are also generally atypical. This is to say, most of them fit the end-scraper and burin definitions only in the crudest sense; they could well be accidents of flint working as opposed to intentional end products.

The sharp predominance of flakes over blades and the great importance of side-scrapers are characteristics that the early Würm and early middle Würm sites of the Ukraine share not only among themselves, but among a large number of other sites of similar age in various parts of Europe, central and southwest Asia, and North Africa. The group of sites sharing these characteristics in the specified time range are generally assigned to the Mousterian culture. Sometimes, especially in the past, *Middle Paleolithic* has been treated as a synonym for *Mousterian*. (Older cultures, the Acheulean, for example, are then lumped in the Lower Paleolithic; more recent cultures, in the Upper Paleolithic.) The shorter term, *Mousterian*, will be the only one used here.

Detailed studies undertaken especially in France (Bordes 1961b) and also in central Europe (Bosinski 1967; Valoch 1968:354-58; 1971:32-36, with references) and southwest Asia (Skinner 1965) have shown that there is considerable variability within the Mousterian. Even among sites that contain basically the same types of tools, the frequencies of these types may vary sharply.

Unfortunately, the number of Mousterian sites in the Ukraine is still too small for a detailed study of variation there. A notion of the kind of variation that probably existed, however, may be obtained by comparing the artifactual contents of Ukrainian sites with those of some other important Mousterian localities in the European USSR (Klein 1966a, 1969a, 1970).

The important extra-Ukrainian sites are an open-air site near Volgograd (formerly Stalingrad) and a group of caves (including especially Kiik-Koba and Starosel'e) in the Crimea.[1] Detailed comparison reveals that the Molodova and Stinka I Mousterian sites on the middle Dnestr contrast with these other localities in containing a significantly smaller proportion of canted side-scrapers, a larger proportion of Levallois flakes, and also a number of sandstone fragments which seem to have been used in grinding hard material, perhaps bone. Sandstone grinders do not occur at the other Mousterian sites in the European USSR. The Molodova localities contrast both with Stinka I and the extra-Ukrainian sites in providing almost no bifacial side-scrapers or other bifacially worked tools, while Stinka I seems to be unique in its especially high percentage of notches and denticulates. Stinka I and the extra-Ukrainian localities vary among themselves in the kinds ond percentages of bifacial tools they contain.

Since the various Soviet Mousterian sites are often separated by great distances, and in many cases by many thousands of years, it seems likely that much, if not most, of the known artifactual variability among them reflects cultural differences among their ancient occupants. In other words, as elsewhere, the Mousterian in the European USSR was not a single undifferentiated culture, but a complex of cultures sharing such features as the manufacture of tools chiefly on flakes and a general preference for side-scrapers of various kinds. Since the environment of the European USSR varied according to both time and space during the early Würm and early middle Würm, it is by no means surprising to find that there were several Mousterian cultures. While it is proper to

---

1. The Crimea is a large lozenge-shaped peninsula jutting into the Black Sea from the southern coast of the Ukraine (map 1). Although it is presently administered as a part of the Ukrainian Soviet Socialist Republic, it is almost always discussed as a distinct unit by physical geographers (for example, Mirov 1951:209-20). Detailed treatments of the Pleistocene prehistory of the Crimea may be found in Klein (1965) and Vekilova (1971).

emphasize this causal relationship, it is also important to point out that some of the variation among Russian Mousterian assemblages may simply reflect differences in the kinds of activities people of a single culture carried out at different sites. This is particularly likely for assemblages coming from sites which may be near in space and time, as, for example, the Mousterian localities on the middle Dnestr.

The number of Mousterian sites on the middle Dnestr has increased significantly in the last few years, and the local abundance of deposits of the right age makes further increase highly probable. In the near future the number may increase to the point where statistical methods may be employed to isolate clusters of tools which were used together. These clusters or "tool kits" show up as sets of tool types whose frequencies of occurrence co-vary from site to site. Pioneer attempts to isolate "tool kits" in the Mousterian of France and the Near East (Binford, L. R., and Binford, S. R., 1966; Binford, S., 1968a; Binford, S. R. and Binford, L. R., 1969) and of Spain (Freeman 1966, and in preparation) have already provided some interesting results. The real information payoff will come if and when correlations are established between "tool kits" and environmental variables such as climate, fauna, and site location. The wealth of environmental data that have come from the middle Dnestr sites make them a particularly promising prospect for future statistical study.

In addition to statements about cultural variability, other interesting conclusions about Mousterian peoples may be drawn from their artifacts, as exemplified in the Ukraine. The very existence of a fairly large variety of identifiable types (more than forty are recognizable in Ukrainian sites), implies that the Mousterians were engaged in a variety of activities. Although the specific functions of the different stone-tool types have not been established, it is clear that some of them must have been used in killing and butchering animals. Scratches and cut marks that were probably made during butchering have been found on bones at various Russian Mousterian sites. Other stone tools were probably used to manufacture artifacts from other substances, for example, hide, wood, and bone. The absence of hide and wood implements at Mousterian localities in the Ukraine and elsewhere is almost certainly a result of their disintegration.

Curiously, although it seems probable that some of the bones that bear signs of cutting and scraping were bone tools, no repetitive bone artifact types are known. In fact, generally speaking, the Mousterian is remarkably poor in clearly recognizable bone implements. In contrast, the people who succeeded the Mousterians in the Ukraine and elsewhere made extraordinary use of bone, producing a variety of objects which are as readily identifiable as the stone-tools. In addition, the successors to the Mousterians frequently used bone and other materials to fashion immediately recognizable art objects. An ochre-stained, polished oval mammoth tooth fragment and a polished invertebrate fossil (nummulite) bearing what appears to be an incised cross are known from the Mousterian site of Tata in Hungary (Vértes 1964:139-42), and some bone fragments with incised macaroni-like patterns have been found in a Mousterian horizon at Cueva Morín in Spain (Freeman 1971:158) and even in an Acheulean horizon at Pech de l'Azé II in southwestern France (Bordes 1972:61-62); but none of these pieces is as clearly artistic in intent as the literally hundreds of objets d'art which have been found in post-Mousterian (Upper Paleolithic) sites in various parts of Europe. The implications of the absence of undoubted art objects in the Mousterian are not entirely clear, but it may constitute evidence that the Mousterians were biopsychologically distinct from later peoples.

Features in Early and Early Middle Würm Sites

Features, that is, irremovable cultural items encountered in excavation, are extremely common in Mousterian sites. Hearths, represented by well-defined lenses of ash and charcoal, have been found in virtually every well-excavated site, including those in the Ukraine. Especially good examples of hearths occur in Mousterian horizons 2, 4, and 5 of Molodova I and horizons 11 and 12 of Molodova V. The thickness of the hearth lenses varies between 0.5 and 3 cm; they are oval in plan and range in size from 20 × 40 cm to 40 × 100 cm (Chernysh 1965).

The near ubiquity of hearths in Mousterian sites, including those in the Ukraine, suggests that Mousterian peoples not only used fire, but may have been capable of making it. Fire for warmth during periods of rest was almost certainly not a luxury, but an absolute necessity, given the very cold conditions which many Mousterian peoples, including those in the Ukraine, had to face. Fire was probably also used in food preparation and perhaps in artifact manufacture (for example, wooden spear points could actually have been hardened by careful exposure to intense heat).

In addition to hearths, horizon 4 of Molodova I provided a spectacular oval arrangement of large mammoth bones (fig. 8). The inner dimensions of the oval were 8 m × 5 m, the outer dimensions 10 m × 7 m. The distance between the inner and outer edges varied from 0.6 to 1.6 m. The area enclosed by the oval contained an immense quantity of cultural debris, including roughly 29,000 pieces of flint, hundreds of fragments of animal bones (food debris), fifteen hearths, and a spot of red ochreous pigment. A. P. Chernysh (1965), whose excavations uncovered the oval, believes it marks the location of an ancient structure. In his opinion, the large bones were probably weights holding down skins stretched over the wooden framework of the structure (fig. 8 presents Chernysh's reconstruction). If Chernysh's interpretation is correct, the ring of bones would constitute the first "ruins" discovered at any Mousterian site. Even if he is wrong, the ring remains the clearest evidence to date for any kind of modification of an open-air site by Mousterian peoples.

A comparable arrangement of large bones has been found in horizon 11 of Molodova V (fig. 9) (Chernysh 1965). It consisted of a rough arc of mammoth bones partially encircling an area 9 m × 7 m. The area contained a large quantity of flint artifacts and fragments of animal bones (food debris) as well as five hearths (out of a total of six in the level). Chernysh believes it is the remnant of a second structure, though patterning is less evident than in the Molodova I bone arrangement.

The occurrence of what may be the remains of structures at Molodova I-4 and Molodova V-11 should come as no surprise. Given the unavailability of natural shelters (caves) and the harsh climate, artificial shelter was probably a prerequisite of survival. It is now known that Mousterian peoples sometimes even modified caves in areas where these were abundant. Examples of modification are the posthole and rubble flooring (pavement) found in Mousterian levels at

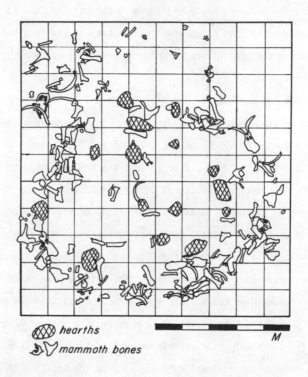

🕸 *hearths*

🦴 *mammoth bones*

M

Fig. 8.--Molodova I, horizon 4. *Above*, circle of large bones; *below*, hypothetical reconstruction of dwelling. (After Chernysh 1965, figs. 18, 23.)

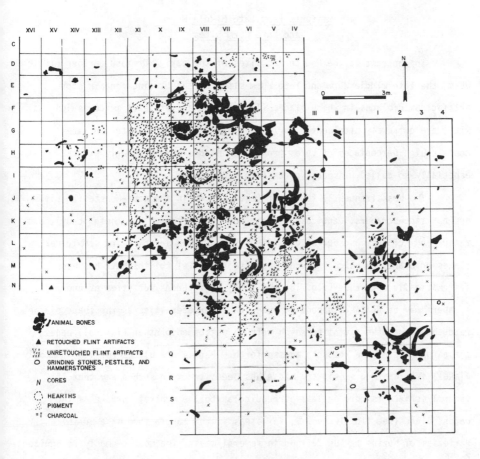

Fig. 9.--Molodova V, horizon 11. Horizontal distribution of cultural debris. (After Chernysh 1965, fig. 55.)

Combe Grenal and La Ferrassie, respectively, in southwestern France (Bordes 1968a: 147; 1972:132-34) and the rubble wall found in Mousterian horizons at Pech de l'Azé I, southwestern France (Bordes 1972:93) and Cueva Morin, northern Spain (Freeman 1971). Even possible examples of cave modification by late ("Riss") Acheulians are known, as at Lazaret, southern France (de Lumley 1969). What now seems remarkable is that such direct evidence for site modification has not been found at more Mousterian sites, particularly ones located in the open. In contrast, "ruins" even more spectacular than those discovered at Molodova I-4 and V-11 are extremely common in the sites of people who occupied Europe after the Mousterians.

Artifacts from Late Middle Würm
and Late Würm Sites

In contrast to the Mousterian sites of the early Würm and earlier middle Würm, the late middle Würm and late Würm sites of the Ukraine contain stone artifact assemblages in which blades (flakes that are at least twice as long as wide) are extremely prominent. Correspondingly, the post-Mousterian sites contain high percentages of cores from which blades were regularly struck, especially so-called prismatic cores (fig. 10, no.1).

The most frequently found retouched pieces in the post-Mousterian sites are not side-scrapers, denticulates, and notches (although all these occur), but rather end-scrapers and burins of various kinds. *End-scrapers* are simply narrow flakes or blades on which the edge opposite (parallel to) the butt has been systematically retouched (fig. 10, nos. 2-5). Different varieties of end-scrapers may be defined, depending upon such characteristics as the shape of the retouched edge, the extent to which retouch passes onto other (lateral) edges, the abruptness of the retouch, and so forth. *Burins* are blades (or less commonly flakes) from which a subsidiary blade has been struck in such a way that its ventral surface is more or less perpendicular to the ventral surface of the parent blade (see fig. 10, no. 6, for steps in the manufacture of a burin). Varieties of burins may be defined in several ways. The most commonly recognized differentiating criterion is the nature of the *striking platform* on the parent blade from which the subsidiary blade, known as a *burin spall*, was struck. For example, the striking platform may consist of a surface formed when a blade was snapped in two. In such a case, we speak of a *burin on the corner of a snapped (broken) blade* (fig. 10, no. 8). Or the striking platform may be formed by very abrupt or truncating retouch on the end of a blade, in which event the resulting burin is known as a *burin on a retouched truncation* (fig. 10, no. 9). Finally, the negative (or scar) left behind by the prior removal of a burin spall in one direction may be used as a striking platform to remove a second spall in another direction (fig. 10, no. 7). The resulting burin is known as a *dihedral burin*. All three major burin types--on the corners of snapped blades, on retouched

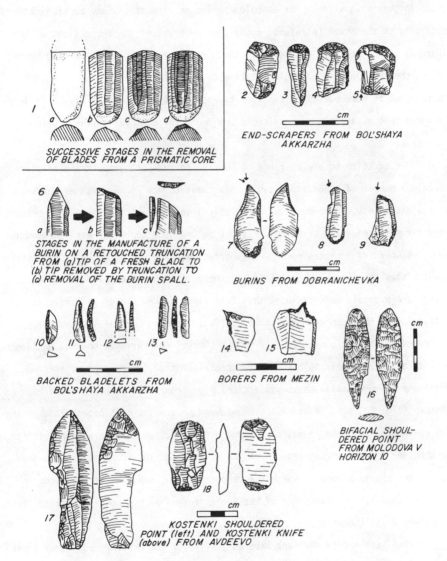

SUCCESSIVE STAGES IN THE REMOVAL
OF BLADES FROM A PRISMATIC CORE

END-SCRAPERS FROM BOL'SHAYA
AKKARZHA

STAGES IN THE MANUFACTURE OF A
BURIN ON A RETOUCHED TRUNCATION
FROM (a) TIP OF A FRESH BLADE TO
(b) TIP REMOVED BY TRUNCATION TO
(c) REMOVAL OF THE BURIN SPALL.

BURINS FROM DOBRANICHEVKA

BACKED BLADELETS FROM
BOL'SHAYA AKKARZHA

BORERS FROM MEZIN

BIFACIAL SHOUL-
DERED POINT
FROM MOLODOVA V
HORIZON 10

KOSTENKI SHOULDERED
POINT (left) AND KOSTENKI KNIFE
(above) FROM AVDEEVO

Fig. 10.--Upper Paleolithic artifacts I. (Nos. 1, 6 after Bordes 1947,
figs. 4,5; 2-5, 7-13 after Boriskovskij and Praslov 1964, pls. 18, 19, 28; 14,
15 after Shovkoplyas 1965b, pls. 27, 28; 16 after Chernysh 1961, fig. 10; 17, 18
after Gvozdover 1961, fig. 51.)

truncations, and dihedral--have been found repeatedly in Ukrainian sites. The three major types can be divided into numerous subtypes which can also be recognized in Ukrainian sites. For example, burins on truncations may be differentiated according to the shape (straight, convex, or concave) of the truncation, while dihedral burins may vary according to the angle formed by the intersecting burin scars, the position of the angle relative to the butt, and so forth. And, of course, two or more burins of the same type or of different types may be manufactured on the same blade, leading to the recognition of yet further burin varieties.

In addition to a wide range of burins and end-scrapers, Ukrainian sites contain a number of other stone tool types, most common among which are backed blades and points. *Backed blades* are simply blades on which one edge has been very abruptly retouched or backed. If the backed edge converges with the opposite edge, we speak of a *backed point*. Very often, backing was produced on relatively small blades known as *bladelets* (fig. 10, nos. 10-13); backed bladelets and points are probably more frequent than full-sized backed pieces in Ukrainian sites. Among the less commonly found artifact types in Ukrainian sites, truncated blades (in many cases, probably "blanks" for burins), borers, shouldered points, and leaf-shaped points deserve special mention. *Borers* are pieces on which one or more small, sharp projections have been deliberately set off by retouch (fig. 10, nos. 14 and 15). *Shouldered points* are most often blades with two converging retouched edges at one end and a notch or unilateral constriction or shoulder made by abrupt retouch at the other (fig. 10, no. 17). *Leaf-shaped points* are simply blades on which the retouched edges converge at both ends (fig. 11, no. 1). At least one of the angles formed by the converging edges must be fairly acute (pointed).

The late middle Würm and late Würm sites of the Ukraine and nearby areas share the prominence of blades and the preference for end-scrapers, burins, backed blades, and other tool types that have been mentioned with sites found elsewhere in Europe, in southwest Asia, and in parts of North Africa in the same time interval. All these sites, or more precisely, the cultural complex they

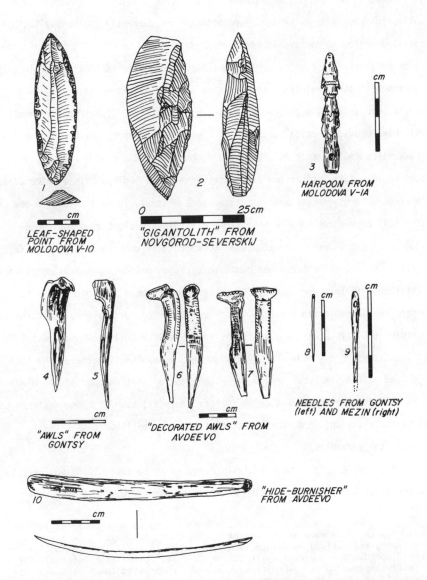

Fig. 11.--Upper Paleolithic artifacts II. (No. 1 after Chernysh 1959, fig. 10; 2 after Boriskovskij 1953, fig. 151; 3, 6, 7 after Abramova 1962, pls. 30, 40; 4, 5, 8 after Boriskovskij and Praslov 1964, pl. 29; 9 after Shovkoplyas 1965b, pl. 44; 10 after Gvozdover 1953, fig. 8.)

comprise, are referred to as "Upper Paleolithic."[2]

Because not all Soviet authors use the same typological concepts or are equally rigorous in applying their concepts, it is currently impossible to obtain a detailed notion of the typological variability among Ukrainian Upper Paleolithic assemblages. In fact, a truly comprehensive idea of variability could only be obtained if the Ukrainian assemblages were to be described according to criteria such as those suggested by Movius et al. (1968). Specifically, Movius et al. have provided logical sets of attributes according to which tools assigned to such major tool classes as end-scrapers, burins, and backed blades may be described in detail. After the attributes of all the tools within a major class in a given assemblage have been tabulated tool by tool, it is possible to use statistical procedures to determine if some attributes cluster on tools non-randomly, that is, more frequently than they would if chance were the only factor dictating their combination. One possible explanation for any nonrandom clusters of attributes is that the ancient toolmaker combined them by choice. Attribute clusters that were formed for this reason could be regarded as true, culturally meaningful tool types, as opposed to the intuitively established types which most prehistorians use today.[3] Obviously, the closer the fit between the tool types used by the prehistorian and those that the ancient knapper had in mind, the more useful the types will be in further analyses, such as those designed to isolate tool kits and to establish correlations between these tool kits and environmental variables.

An example of attribute analysis provided by Sackett (1966) may help to make the procedure clearer. Working with end-scrapers from the French Upper

---

2. Sometimes *Upper Paleolithic* has been used as a synonym for late middle Würm and late Würm as defined here. Used in this way, it is not only superfluous, but misleading, since it may be taken to imply that the entire occupied world shared certain basic cultural traits during this interval. This is clearly an unwarranted assumption. In areas such as southern Asia and sub-Saharan Africa, the late Würm contemporaries of the Upper Paleolithic peoples of Europe, southwest Asia, and North Africa have left behind artifact assemblages which are quite distinctive. Even in Siberia, directly adjacent to the European USSR on the east, the local late Würm cultures should not be referred to as Upper Paleolithic without a modifying epithet (Klein 1971).

3. The most widely used set of intuitively defined Upper Paleolithic tool types are those which have been clearly and concisely set forth by de Sonneville-Bordes and Perrot (1954-56).

Paleolithic (Aurignacian) site of Castanet, Sackett found that pieces with particularly well-rounded scraping fronts had marginal (lateral) retouch more frequently than if "roundedness of scraping front" (measured objectively according to a method Sackett describes) and the presence or absence of marginal retouch were distributed among tools by chance alone. The implication is that these two attributes were somehow causally linked when the Castanet end-scrapers were being manufactured. In this particular instance, mechanical contingencies over which the manufacturer had no control may have been more important than personal (cultural) choice in causing attribute linkage, but the principle behind attribute analysis is still illustrated.

Attribute analysis is now underway in the Soviet Union, but it will probably be many years before it will provide data for a comprehensive assessment of the variability among Upper Paleolithic collections from the Ukraine and nearby areas. Sufficient information from traditional intuitive descriptions is available, however, to show that significant typological variability among collections does exist (Grigor'ev 1970). As in the case of the Mousterian, much of the variability is quantitative, that is, it is reflected in different frequencies of the same types at different sites. In some instances, as, for example, among the roughly contemporaneous sites clustered on the middle Dnestr, such type-frequency variation may only reflect variation in the kinds of activities that people of the same culture carried out at different sites. In other cases, where simple frequency variation is overshadowed by absolute differences in the presence or absence of important types, and where the sites involved are widely separated in time or space, it is likely that the sites were occupied by people of different cultures. Thus, for example, the presence of completely bifacial shouldered points in Molodova V, horizon 10 (fig. 10, no. 16), and their absence at all other Ukrainian sites clearly suggests that Molodova V-10 was derived from a different culture than the other sites.

Distinctive stone artifact types have also been found at Novgorod-Severskij on the Desna and at Avdeevo on the Sejm. At Novgorod-Severskij, they consist of three so-called gigantoliths, massive chipped flint artifacts weighing 4550, 8050, and 8250 grams, respectively (Boriskovskij 1953:293), of which at least two are enormous multifaceted burins (fig. 11, no. 2). At Avdeevo, the distinctive stone artifacts belong to two types--so-called Kostenki knives and Kostenki points (Gvozdover 1958:31-76; 1961). The *Kostenki Knives* are blades or flakes on which the butt and the edge opposite it have been truncated by abrupt retouch on the ventral surface (fig. 10, no. 18). *Kostenki Points* are shouldered points on which both the shoulder and the point were formed largely on the dorsal surface, the shoulder by abrupt retouch (fig. 10, no. 17). Very frequently, the point or the base of the shoulder bear ventral retouch as well. Kostenki points and knives derive their name from their prominence in the uppermost level of the site of Kostenki I on the Don, 210 km southeast of Avdeevo (map 2) (Klein 1969b: 116-40).

Kostenki I-1, its sister site of Kostenki XVIII, which also contains both Kostenki points and knives (Klein 1969b:140-41), and Avdeevo have been lumped into the "Kostenki-Avdeevo culture." The appropriateness of this assignment is underlined by the similarities between Avdeevo and Kostenki I-1 in other artifact types (especially art objects described delow) and in features (see also below). In fact, these similarities are so striking that it is even possible to imagine that the occupants of the two sites belonged to the same identity-conscious group. Certainly, at the very least, they belonged to two very closely related groups.

The case of Kostenki I-1 and Avdeevo remains the best instance in the European USSR for assigning two fairly distant early man sites to the same culture in the narrow, ethnographic sense of the word. Kostenki points by themselves, without the other distinctive artifacts and features of the Kostenki-Avdeevo culture, have been found in Upper Paleolithic sites as far away as Czechoslovakia and Austria. They may also occur at Berdyzh on the Sozh (Polikarpovich 1968:26; Bud'ko et al. 1971). What, if any, cultural significance this rather far-flung distribution has, remains unclear.

Although, as with Mousterian artifacts, Upper Paleolithic stone tools in the Ukraine and elsewhere have been given names which suggest that their functions are known, in fact this is not the case. The true functions of the overwhelming majority of implements can only be guessed at. Soviet scientists

in particular have sought to reduce the guesswork by studying the traces of
utilization sometimes preserved on Upper Paleolithic artifacts (see especially
Semenov 1964). So far, however, they have met with only limited success. For
example, in the case of the Kostenki points, they have found that many specimens
display intensive edge wear (striations, polishing, chipping) more suggestive
of tools that were in repeated and prolonged use (as household utensils, for
example) than of weapons. It may therefore be argued that Kostenki points were
not used to arm projectiles, but the range of uses to which they could have been
put remains large.

It is interesting to point out that traces of wear are commonly found on
unretouched pieces. For example, microscopic examination of several unretouched
blades from Pushkari I showed that their edges were polished and striated. The
wear occurred on both the ventral and dorsal surfaces, suggesting that the
blades were used for cutting rather than for scraping. The possibility that
unretouched blades were used for cutting is not surprising when it is realized
that a fresh flint edge is actually sharper than a retouched one. Retouch in
fact blunts an edge and in most cases was probably done to give the edge a
desired shape or to reduce its fragility and brittleness. Obviously, reduced
brittleness would have been especially desirable on tools that were used for
scraping. Microscopic examination of the retouched edges of end-scrapers from
Pushkari I showed that all observable wear was confined to the dorsal surface
(Boriskovskij 1953:205ff). This may be taken as evidence that the retouched
edges were in fact used for scraping rather than for cutting.

In addition to stone tool types, the Upper Paleolithic sites of the
Ukraine, like Upper Paleolithic sites elsewhere (and in contrast to the previously discussed Mousterian sites), often contain abundant and easily recognizable
artifacts of bone, ivory, or antler. Sometimes, as for example the antler
"harpoons" of Molodova V, horizons 1 and 1A (fig. 11, no. 3), these artifacts
belong to types which seem to be restricted to only one or two sites. Such
unique artifacts serve to reinforce the notion that the Upper Paleolithic of the
Ukraine, like the Upper Paleolithic elsewhere, comprised a number of similar
cultures varying in time and space. In addition to bone-ivory-antler artifacts,

which occur in only one or two sites, there are several types which have been found at a number of sites. These types vary in frequency of occurrence and often in details of manufacture (as would be expected if they were frequently made by members of different cultures), but they share enough characteristics to allow the establishment of types. These recurrent bone-ivory-antler artifacts are awls, needles, shaft-straighteners, hide-burnishers, projectile points, antler hammers, digging tools, and bone hafts.

Awls are usually limb bones of small animals with one end sharpened to a point and the other consisting of an intact articular head (fig. 11, nos. 4, 5). *Needles* are generally thin slivers of bone or ivory with one end sharpened to a point and the other pierced by a small hole (the "eye") (fig. 11, nos. 8, 9). Awls and needles may have been used to manufacture clothing and other artifacts of leather and fur. Certainly, the cold conditions in which Upper Paleolithic peoples lived in the Ukraine and elsewhere demanded well-made clothing.

Shaft-straighteners from Ukrainian sites are primarily artifacts cut from bone or ivory whose appearance recalls large, dull skewers or tent pegs (fig. 12, nos. 1, 2). They consist of two principal parts: a broad end pierced by a large hole, and a long shaft. Their function in the Ukraine, as elsewhere, remains unclear. They have variously been interpreted as shaft wrenches, thong-stroppers, and status symbols (*"batons-de-commandement"*); even the tent-peg possibility cannot be ruled out.

Hide-burnishers are long, flat strips of bone (usually ribs of medium-sized animals like horse or reindeer) on which one end has been given a convex shape and subsequently polished or even bevelled (fig. 11, no. 10). As the name suggests, it is widely believed that these artifacts were used to burnish hides.

Projectile points are rods of bone or ivory on which one end has been sharpened or polished to a point (fig. 12, nos. 3, 4). Such artifacts may have been used to tip spears with, possibly, wooden shafts. At some sites--for example, Mezin (Shovkoplyas 1965b), Molodova V-3 (Chernysh 1959), and Amvrosievka (Boriskovskij and Praslov 1964)--longitudinal grooves were incised into some projectile points, perhaps to serve as blood runnels or slots for the insertion

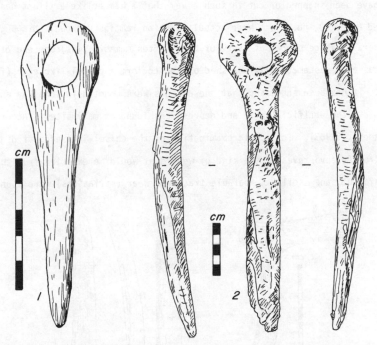

"SHAFT-STRAIGHTENERS" FROM MEZIN (left) AND MOLODOVA V-HORIZON 7 (right)

GROOVED "PROJECTILE POINT" FROM MEZIN

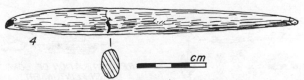

PROJECTILE POINT FROM AMVROSIEVKA

Fig. 12.--Upper Paleolithic artifacts III. (Nos. 1, 3 after Shovkoplyas 1965b, pl. 45; 2 after Abramova 1962, pl. 40; 4 after Boriskovskij and Praslov 1964, pl. 40.)

of flint artifacts, possibly backed bladelets.

Antler hammers are fragments of antler (mainly reindeer) from which tines have been snapped or cut in such a way that a hammerlike artifact has resulted (fig. 13, no. 1). Their actual function remains unknown. *Digging tools* are generally large pieces of ivory or bone (often mammoth ribs) one end of which has been systematically polished or cut to form a chisel-like edge (fig. 13, no. 2). It has been suggested that these tools were mounted in some way and used to dig the artificial pits and depressions found at many sites. According to Gvozdover (1953), microscopic examination of the chisel-like ends of digging tools from Avdeevo revealed the kind of wear that would be expected from the excavation of sandy soil. Comparable traces of wear (striations) were found on

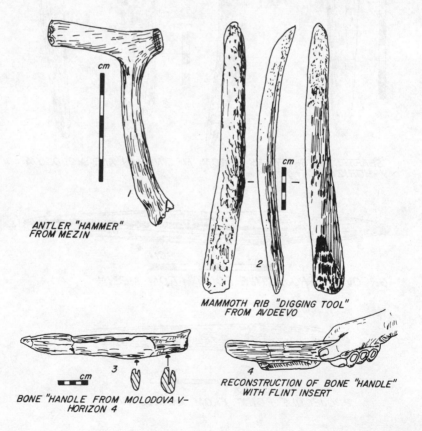

cm

ANTLER "HAMMER"
FROM MEZIN

cm

MAMMOTH RIB "DIGGING TOOL"
FROM AVDEEVO

cm

BONE "HANDLE FROM MOLODOVA V-
HORIZON 4

RECONSTRUCTION OF BONE "HANDLE"
WITH FLINT INSERT

Fig. 13.--Upper Paleolithic artifacts IV. (No. 1 after Shovkoplyas 1965b: pl. 39; 2 after Gvozdover 1953, fig. 5; 3, 4 after Chernysh 1961, figs. 22, 36.)

a digging tool from Pushkari I(Boriskovskij 1953:223).

Finally, *bone hafts* or handles consist of pieces of ivory, bone, or antler which have been grooved or slotted, presumably for the insertion of flint elements (fig. 13, nos. 3, 4). In some cases it is possible that the splinters of bone or antler removed from the grooves were the object of the exercise; in such instances the bone "hafts" may constitute nothing more than discarded sources of raw material for other artifacts.

At several sites, bone artifacts belonging to the supposedly utilitarian types that have been described exhibit patterns of incised lines which suggest decoration. Both the shafts and the heads of several awls found at Avdeevo carried systematically incised lines or small crosses (fig. 11, nos. 6, 7). Similar decoration was found on the margins of some Avdeevo "hide-burnishers" and on other bone and ivory artifacts (Gvozdover 1953). The tendency to engrave geometric patterns on bone-ivory-antler artifacts seems to have characterized the occupants of many Ukrainian Upper Paleolithic sites, though the precise pattern they favored varies. At Eliseevichi, for example, in contrast to Avdeevo, a net-like or beehive-like design (fig. 14, no. 1) is very common (Abramova 1962: 45-47), while the people of Mezin clearly preferred chevron or herring bone decoration, often in combination with angular spirals (fig. 14, no. 6; fig. 15, no. 1).

In addition to geometrically "decorated" bone-ivory-antler artifacts, many Ukrainian Upper Paleolithic sites, like Upper Paleolithic sites elsewhere, contained objects which were clearly art objects or ornaments in the narrow sense. Among the ornaments, "beads" and "pendants" consisting of marine shells pierced by a hole (fig. 14, nos. 2, 3) or teeth of the arctic fox and wolf, each with a hole drilled through the root (fig. 14, nos. 4, 5), are especially common. The art objects vary enormously from site to site, documenting more clearly than any other artifact type the occurrence of several Upper Paleolithic cultures in the Ukraine and nearby regions. For example, only the site of Molodova V-7 has so far provided a shaft-straightener with what seems to be a human figure engraved on it (fig. 12, no. 2). Mezin, in contrast, is unique for its two "bracelets," consisting in one case of a single curved ivory blade with an

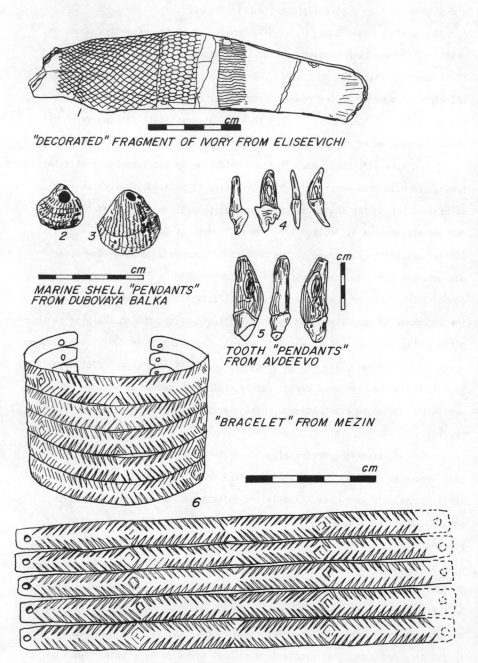

"DECORATED" FRAGMENT OF IVORY FROM ELISEEVICHI

MARINE SHELL "PENDANTS" FROM DUBOVAYA BALKA

TOOTH "PENDANTS" FROM AVDEEVO

"BRACELET" FROM MEZIN

Fig. 14.--Upper Paleolithic artifacts V. (No. 1 after Efimenko 1953, fig. 260; 2, 3 after Boriskovskij and Praslov 1964, pl. 22; 4, 5 after Abramova 1962, pl. 30; 6 after Shovkoplyas 1965b, pl. 52.)

incised pattern of interrelated spirals and zigzags, and in the second case of
five separate, similarly curled ivory blades which, when placed together (they
were found together), exhibit a surficial zigzag or herring bone pattern (fig.
14, no. 6). Mezin also contained some unique ivory objects, perhaps depicting
birds with folded wings (fig. 15, no. 1), and some enigmatic pieces interpreted
as phallic symbols (fig. 15, no. 2). The surfaces of these and other objects
frequently bear the incised herringbone and spiral pattern which is a hallmark
of Mezin. Finally, Mezin is nearly unique in containing several large mammoth
bones on which geometric patterns have been painted with red ochre (fig. 15, nos.
3, 4). Only Mezhirich has also provided painted mammoth bones, in this case with
a "line and dot" pattern.

Unique and interesting art objects have also been found at several other
Ukrainian sites of which Eliseevichi and Avdeevo are probably the best examples.
Eliseevichi contained a fragmentary figurine from which the head and arms had
been broken off (fig. 16, no. 1). Obvious breasts and prominent buttocks clearly
indicate it was intended to depict a woman. It is broadly reminiscent of female
statuettes ("venus figurines") known from Upper Paleolithic sites in various
parts of Europe. Avdeevo contained four human figurines, of which two represent
roughcasts in the initial stages of manufacture, while two others are more nearly
finished products. These latter two are similar to completed Upper Paleolithic
figurines found elsewhere in that they are highly schematic (fig. 16, nos. 4, 5).
The head in each case is rendered as a round blob without face or hair. The
arms and legs are similarly presented without detail. The presence of breasts
on one of the figurines indicates that it was intended to portray a female.
Neither of the more-or-less finished figurines possesses realistic proportions,
one being excessively squat and stocky, the other overly long and lanky.

In addition to human statuettes, Avdeevo contained a stylized mammoth
figurine in soft bone (fig. 16, no. 2) and several enigmatic art objects, including some elaborate "hide-burnisher"-like pieces. The latter (all fragmentary)
are long strips of bone one end of which has been carved to resemble an animal
head while the other end is presumed to have been bevelled in the fashion of a
"burnisher" (fig. 16, no. 3). The "head" is pierced by up to four small holes,

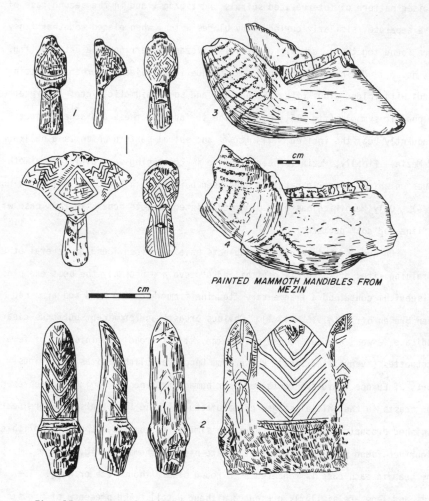

PAINTED MAMMOTH MANDIBLES FROM
MEZIN

Fig. 15.--Upper Paleolithic artifacts VI.   No. 1, "bird" statuette from Mezin; no. 2, "phallic symbol" from Mezin. (After Abramova 1962 pls. 31, 32, 35.)

while both the head and the shaft frequently carry the evenly spaced, short incised lines or crosses often found on the margins of other Avdeevo artifacts. The Avdeevo art objects which have been described, and some which have not, may be matched nearly piece for piece with art objects from Kostenki I-1 (Klein 1969b:122-40). This serves to reinforce the notion that Avdeevo and Kostenki I-1 were occupied by people belonging to a single cultural tradition.

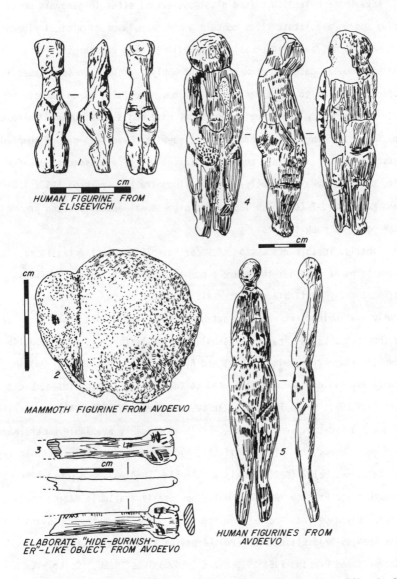

HUMAN FIGURINE FROM
ELISEEVICHI

MAMMOTH FIGURINE FROM AVDEEVO

ELABORATE "HIDE-BURNISH-
ER"-LIKE OBJECT FROM AVDEEVO

HUMAN FIGURINES FROM
AVDEEVO

Fig. 16.--Upper Paleolithic artifacts VII. (No. 1 after Efimenko 1953, fig. 261; 2 - 6 after Abramova 1962, pls. 27, 29.)

Like Upper Paleolithic (and also Mousterian) sites in general, most
Ukrainian Upper Paleolithic sites contain grains and lumps of mineral pigment
(ochre, mainly red, but also occasionally yellow). The reasons that Upper
Paleolithic peoples gathered pigment were probably various. In some cases it
undoubtedly was used to paint designs on various materials, as on mammoth bones
at Mezin and Mezhirich. In other cases it may have had a more mundane purpose,
perhaps in the tanning of leather. Pigment seems to have been ground to powder
on sandstone tablets which are known from several sites. At some sites--for
example, Dobranichevka (Shovkoplyas 1970), Timonovka II (Grekhova 1968; 1969:95-
96), and Molodova V-7 (Chernysh 1961)--red pigment was actually found ground
into the pores of such tablets.

Finally, in this discussion of Upper Paleolithic artifacts, it is
important to point out that there are a number of sites in which artifacts
made of nonlocally available raw materials have been found. For example,
nonlocally available flint was used extensively to manufacture stone tools at
Gontsy (Boriskovskij and Praslov 1964:34), Gorodok II (Boriskovskij 1953:145-47),
Yudinovo (Polikarpovich 1968:166-67), and Avdeevo (Gvozdover 1958:31-33).
Nonlocally available stone was also used at Voronovista I-1 (obsidian, see
Chernysh 1959:196), Babin I-1 (radiolarite, see Chernysh 1959:196), and Ataki-
Kel'menets I-3 (quartz, see Chernysh 1968a). Nonlocally available amber, manu-
factured into "beads" and other artifacts, has been found at Mezin (Shovkoplyas
1965b), Kajstrova balka (Boriskovskij and Praslov 1964:29), and Dobranichevka
(Boriskovskij and Praslov 1964:33), while nonlocally available marine shells,
also frequently made into "beads" and "pendants," are known from Dubovaya balka
(Kolosov 1964:46-47), Eliseevichi (Polikarpovich 1968), Kajstrova balka
(Boriskovskij and Praslov 1964:29), Mezin (Shovkoplyas 1965b), Osokorovka I
(Kolosov 1964:46), Yudinovo (Polikarpovich 1968:166-67), and Timonovka
(Polikarpovich 1968).

In some cases it is possible to estimate the distance over which a nonlocally available raw material may have moved. Thus, no natural occurrences of
amber are known within 150 km of the site of Dobranichevka, while the closest
exposure of obsidian to Voronovitsa I is 300 km away; and the marine shells found

at Yudinovo almost certainly had to come a minimum of 680 km--from the modern
Black Sea coast or perhaps from deposits of the Last (Karangat) Transgression of
the Black Sea. The means by which materials, or perhaps even finished artifacts,
moved over relatively great distances are not understood, though such movement
seems to have been a fairly common occurrence in the Upper Paleolithic (see, for
example, Klein 1969b:227). Comparable movements do not seem to have occurred in
the Mousterian.

Comparison of Ukrainian Upper Paleolithic artifact assemblages with
contemporaneous assemblages from elsewhere in Europe suggests that the cultures
which are represented were more or less restricted to the Ukraine and its
immediate neighbors. Soviet investigators and others have sometimes under-
estimated the originality of their materials and have described them with
cultural terms like Aurignacian, Solutrean, and Magdalenian, which have their
principal application in western Europe, especially in France (see, for example,
de Sonneville-Bordes 1963). Sometimes the Ukrainian sites have been lumped
with others in eastern and central Europe into the "Eastern Gravettian."
Whichever practice is followed--applying western European labels to the Ukrainian
cultures or lumping them into one culture--the same basic mistake is made. The
extensive variability which is a major characteristic of the Ukrainian Upper
Paleolithic is thereby masked. As elsewhere, the extent to which the Ukrainian
Upper Paleolithic varied in time and space far exceeds the obvious spatial and
temporal variability within the Mousterian. This greater apparent internal
diversity is one of the major features by which the Upper Paleolithic may be
distinguished from the Mousterian.

Features in Late Middle Würm and Late Würm Sites

As do the Mousterian sites which antedate them, Upper Paleolithic sites
in the Ukraine and environs generally contain clear-cut lenses of ash and charcoal interpreted as the remains of hearths. Often the hearths are incorporated
as parts of complex features which are widely accepted as ruins. The most
spectacular "ruins" have been found at sites in the Dnepr-Desna drainage. They

consist mainly of patterned arrangements of mammoth bones, sometimes in association with other evidence for structural modification, such as artificially dug
depressions. A few sites in the Dnepr-Desna drainage, and several on the middle
Dnestr, contain ruins in which arrangements of postholes, depressions, or
sharply bounded concentrations of cultural debris are the most conspicuous
elements.

It must be emphasized that the discovery of ruins requires very careful
excavation procedures in which the positions of all important classes of debris
are plotted horizontally across the surface of a site. If possible, it is
generally best to leave major items in place while further debris are being
uncovered. This allows an immediate visual assessment of spatial patterning.
In the first few decades of early man research (from roughly the 1860s until
1930), such procedures were rarely, if ever, employed. The emphasis was on the
stratigraphic (vertical) positions of excavated materials (Sackett 1968:66ff.),
and it is possible that the ruins which were present at many sites were simply
not recognized. Following the first discovery of Pleistocene ruins at the
Upper Paleolithic site of Gagarino on the Don River in 1927 (Zamyatnin 1929) and
the consequent realization that such ruins might be a common feature of Pleistocene sites, Soviet investigators began to employ horizontally oriented excavation
procedures. They pioneered such techniques, which in fact did not become common
in other parts of Europe until the last decade or two. The early application of
appropriate excavation methods is perhaps the main reason why the Ukraine is
relatively rich in spectacular ruins.

Patterned accumulations of mammoth bones regarded as the remains of
structures have been uncovered at Berdyzh (Bud'ko 1964; Bud'ko et al. 1971),
Dobranichevka (Pidoplichko 1969:69-76; Shovkoplyas 1970), Eliseevichi (Polikarpovich
1968:53-64; Bud'ko and Sorokina 1969:131), Gontsy (Boriskovskij and Praslov 1964:
35), Kirillovskaya (Pidoplichko 1969:40), Mezhirich (Pidoplichko 1969:111-44),
Mezin (Shovkoplyas 1965b), Radomyshl' (Shovkoplyas 1965a), Suponevo (Boriskovskij
1958:12; Gromov 1948:140), and Yudinovo(Bud'ko 1967; Bud'ko and Sorokina 1969:
133-34; Polikarpovich 1968:140; Rogachev 1964:7-8).

At *Berdyzh*, large mammoth bones, some standing nearly upright, were found ringing an artificial depression 9-10 m long, 3-4 m wide, and 40-50 cm deep. The depression contained a large quantity of stone artifacts and broken-up animal remains surrounding a roughly oval hearth. Unfortunately, the depression and its contents were not recognized as ruins at the time of excavation; as a consequence, they were not accurately plotted over the surface of the site. Only a rough plan, reconstructed from field notes, is available (fig. 17). It shows that in addition to the main depression, Berdyzh contained three bone-filled pits which may have been building-material or fuel caches. The pits were 1-2 m across and up to 60 cm deep. One occurred on the floor of the large depression; the other two were located outside it. Additional mammoth bone features found at Berdyzh in recent years have not been illustrated in print, but are said to form part of the complex shown schematically in figure 17.

At *Dobranichevka*, the ruins consist principally of four rings of select, upright mammoth bones. The rings were scattered over an area of several hundred square meters and were never less than 20 m apart. Each had a diameter of about 4 m and surrounded an area in which additional large bones occurred. The only ring for which an illustration is available (fig. 18) was incomplete, due to partial destruction by recent highway construction. It did not contain a clear-cut hearth, although one thin, ashy lens (diameter 40 cm), charred bones, and scattered ashy particles suggest that fires burned inside it. One of the other rings did contain a well-defined lens of ash and charcoal in a shallow, dish-shaped depression 70 cm across. Two additional hearths were found immediately outside this ring. Also outside the rings, but presumably in association with them, were ten large pits, nine of which were filled with bones (belonging mainly to mammoth). The one bone-filled pit which has been illustrated (fig. 18) was 2 m across the top, 1.7 m across the bottom, and approximately 1.2 m deep. The single pit that did not contain large bones (fig. 18) was filled mainly by stone artifacts, bits of ochre, pieces of amber (some made into beads), and bone splinters, including many that were charred. This pit measured 2 m across the top, 1.3 m across the bottom, and 90 cm in depth. A 45 centimeter-deep channel ran out from one side of it, perhaps to a hearth which the road crew may have accidentally destroyed.

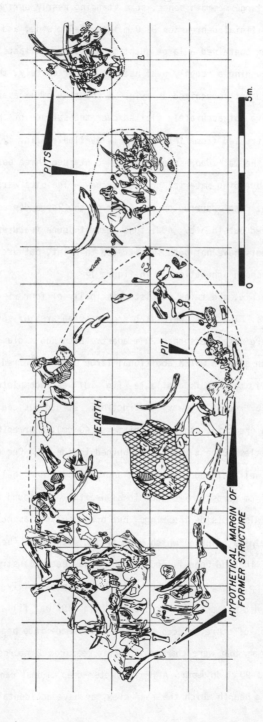

Fig. 17.--Berdyzh. Plan of the 1938-39 excavations showing the distribution of large bones and the principal features. (After Bud'ko 1964, fig. 7.)

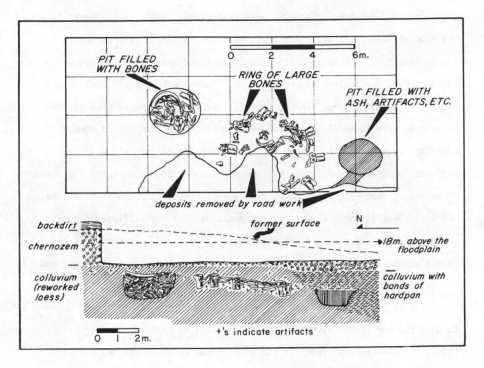

Fig. 18.--Dobranichevka. Plan and profile of one of the major complexes of features. (After Boriskovskij and Praslov 1964, pl. 28.)

The principal mammoth bone features found at *Eliseevichi* were some bone-filled pits, an oval concentration of tusks and fragmentary scapulae covering a 3-4 m^2 area, and two subparallel rows of large mammoth bones, mainly pelves and scapulae, frequently standing vertically. Beneath the oval concentration was a lens of ash and charcoal 85 cm in diameter. The length of each of the two rows of large bones was 6.5 m. The distance between them varied from 1 to 1.5 m. The horizontal relationship between the two major mammoth bone features has not been clarified in print, nor is it entirely clear how they stood relative to a large oval depression which constitutes the remaining evidence for structural modification at Eliseevichi. This depression measured 9.4 × 8.8 m across and was up to 60 cm deep. It contained a large quantity of cultural debris, some in a steep-sided oval pit dug into the middle bottom of the depression.

Excavations at *Gontsy* uncovered several concentrations of mammoth bones and associated hearths. Since the principal excavations were conducted before the days of horizontal plots, no reliable illustrations of the concentrations are available. The verbal description of at least one, however, suggests structural ruins. The central element in these "ruins" was an oval, bowl-shaped depression, 6 × 4 m across and up to 40 cm deep. Along the margins of the depression were found 24 mammoth skulls and perhaps as many as 30 mammoth scapulae, several of which stood vertically. Three additional skulls, several scapulae, numerous tusks, and other mammoth remains occurred inside the depression in positions that suggest collapse from a superstructure. The floor of the depression was littered with artifacts and broken-up bones of various animals, concentrated around a single hearth. Eight steep-sided, circular pits 1.2-2 m across and 60-70 cm deep occurred just outside the depression. Each pit contained from 5 to 11 mammoth tusks and a variety of other bones and artifacts.

Like Gontsy, *Kirillovskaya* was excavated before it had become commonplace to plot the horizontal distributions of cultural materials. However, it is known that the lower (second) level of the site contained three roughly circular concentrations of bones in which mammoth skulls, mandibles, and tusks played the major role. By analogy with other Ukrainian sites, these concentrations may be regarded as the remnants of structures. At least one concentration was associated with a lens of ash and charcoal 2-3 m in diameter.

Recent excavations at the site of *Mezhirich* have provided some of the best-described and most spectacular bone "ruins" so far found in the Ukraine. These consisted of 385 mammoth bones covering a roughly circular area 4-5 m across (fig. 19). When the bones were removed, the area underneath provided 4600 flint artifacts and numerous other cultural debris scattered around a circular pit 50 cm in diameter and 20 cm deep. The pit was filled with ash and charcoal and may have been a hearth. Some large bones standing vertically alongside it perhaps formed part of a barbecue apparatus. Two additional hearths, 2-3 m across and up to 15 cm thick, were found beyond the margins of the ruins.

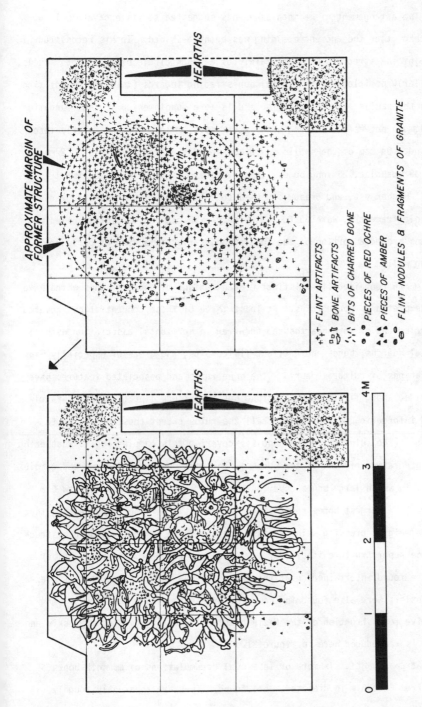

Fig. 19.--Mezhirich. *Left*, mass of mammoth bones representing constructional material from ruined dwelling; *right*, distribution of cultural debris over the floor of the dwelling. (After Pidoplichko 1969, figs. 43, 48.)

The arrangement of mammoth bones has suggested to its excavator, I. G. Pidoplichko, that the ancient building was beehive-shaped. In his reconstruction, the base of the structure consists mainly of a rough circle of 25 mammoth skulls, all similarly positioned with frontal bones facing inwards (this is the position in which the skulls were found). The skulls were supplemented in the foundation by 20 mammoth pelves and 10 long bones stuck more or less perpendicularly into the ground. On top of the skulls and other foundation bones were laid 12 more skulls, 30 scapulae, 20 long bones, 15 pelves, and segments of 7 vertebral columns. Higher yet, and presumably used to hold down skins stretched over a wooden-pole framework, were 35 tusks. Ninety-five mammoth mandibles, piled up in columns around a portion of the foundation, served as a kind of peripheral retaining wall.

Mezin contained five distinct concentrations of mammoth bones which have been interpreted as house ruins. At least three of these concentrations covered or encircled one or more hearths and occurred in horizontal association with additional hearths, bone- and artifact-filled pits, and areas of especially high concentrations of cultural debris. The bone ruins and associated features have been divided among five complexes strung out in a rough line (fig. 20). Fairly detailed information is available on all the ruins except those belonging to complex 5. (The thinness of the deposits covering this complex led to weathering and disintegration of many of the bones.) The most completely documented complex is no. 1, in which large bones covered a shallow, roughly circular hollow 6 m in diameter. The largest bones tended to occur near the periphery, suggesting that they were weights pressing skins against the base of a now collapsed superstructure. The superstructure itself may have included reindeer antlers, a number of which were found intertwined near the center of the bone concentration (intertwined antlers were also found in the ruins of the remaining complexes). An imaginative reconstruction of the Mezin complex 1 dwelling as a conical skin and bone hut is reproduced here in figure 21.

At *Radomyshl'*, six more or less oval accumulations of mammoth bones, ranging from 3 to 6 m in diameter, were found. They are apparently roughly similar to those found at Mezin and have been interpreted similarly. A round

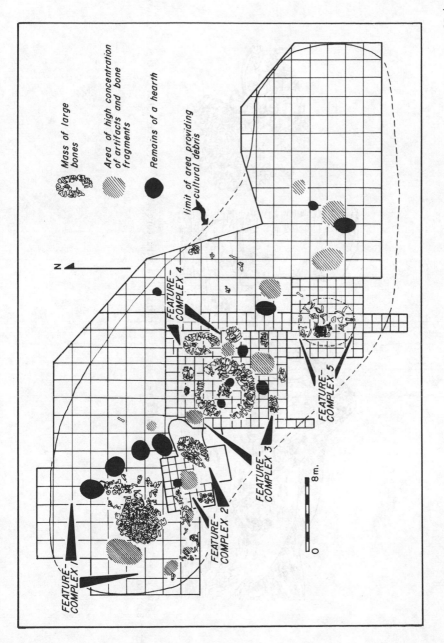

Fig. 20.--Mezin. Horizontal relationship of the major complexes of features. (After Shovkoplyas 1965b, fig. 15.)

Fig. 21.--Mezin. *Right*, mass of bones representing ruins of a structure, *left*, reconstruction of the structure. (After Boriskovskij 1958, fig. 1.)

pit 2 m across and 1 m deep, filled with tusks and other mammoth bones, was associated with them. Comparable mammoth bone features also apparently occurred at *Suponevo*, though detailed documentation is lacking.

Finally, *Yudinovo* contained at least two spectacular and perhaps unique sets of bone "ruins," which unfortunately have not yet been clearly illustrated. The first set was composed of two concentric rings of large bones. The outer ring was more or less continuous and consisted of more than 20 mammoth skulls as well as a large number of mammoth long bones, scapulae, and pelves. Its diameter was approximately 9.5 m. The inner ring was discontinuous and was made up almost exclusively of mammoth skulls (14 in total). Its diameter was 7.5 m. Inside the inner ring were additional mammoth scapulae, pelves, and long bones. Many of the scapulae and pelves were perforated by holes, as if they were meant to receive posts. An oval (2.15 × 2 m) lens of ash and charcoal was found inside the inner ring.

The second Yudinovo mammoth bone feature was centered on a large depression surrounded by 56 mammoth skulls and other large bones, some standing upright or resting on one another. Linear arrangements of large bones within the depression divide it into six separate sections (rooms?).

Eight sites contain ruins of structures in which mammoth bones are not the most conspicuous elements. These are Pushkari I (Boriskovskij 1953:179-228), Lipa I (Savich 1968), Avdeevo (Rogachev 1953:143-87), Molodova V, horizons 7, 6, 3, and 2 (Chernysh 1959, 1961), and Voronovitsa I, horizon 1 (Chernysh 1959: 46-51).

Excavations at *Pushkari I* uncovered an irregularly quadrangular shallow depression roughly 12 m long, 4 m wide, and 30 cm deep (fig. 22). Three evenly spaced lenses of ash and charcoal (hearths) were found on a line dividing the depression into two long halves. The hearths were surrounded by a series of small pits, variously interpreted as caches and postholes. Some of the possible postholes contained splinters of bone driven into the ground, perhaps as support wedges. The floor of the depression was littered with stone artifacts, bits of ochre, and broken-up animal bones. Overlying the floor were a large number of mammoth bones, especially tusks, perhaps part of a collapsed superstructure.

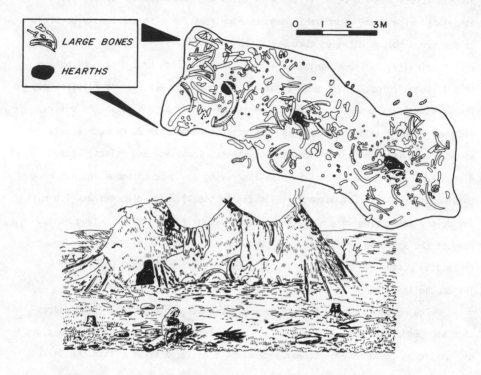

Fig. 22.--Pushkari I. *Above*, floor plan of the "ruins"; *below*, reconstruction of the dwelling. (After Boriskovskij 1958, fig. 3.)

The principal excavator of Pushkari I, P. I. Boriskovskij, believes the building
was composed of three separate parts, each centered around a hearth. His
interesting, though admittedly speculative reconstruction depicts an amalgamation
of three distinct, conical, teepee-like huts (fig. 22).

Lipa I contained a roughly circular depression 3.6-3.65 m across with a
hearth and what are possibly cache pits on its floor. No illustrations or
further details are available.

Avdeevo contained an extraordinary complex of features centered on a
huge lens of dark (ochre-colored) sandy silt covering approximately 500 m^2.
Erosion had destroyed a large portion of this lens prior to excavation. Assuming
that it was oval in plan, it may originally have covered an area of 800 m^2 (with
major axis 45 m and minor axis about 20 m). The overwhelming majority of
cultural debris (artifacts and bones) found at Avdeevo were located within the

confines of the dark lens. Fifteen large pits, separated into two basic types, occurred along its periphery. Pits of the first type (designated by the capital letters A-G in fig. 23) covered irregular areas of 4-8 m^2. Each had relatively sheer sides and a maximum depth of 80-100 cm. In each case, on the bottom there was 20-25 cm of ochre colored silt chock-full of artifacts and broken-up bones; near the top was a series of large mammoth bones. It is believed the large bones came from the superstructure which once covered each pit. The pits themselves have been interpreted as sleeping chambers.

The second type of large peripheral pits were smaller and more regular in outline than the "sleeping chambers," though they also had sheer sides and depths from 60 to 100 cm. (They are designated by the Roman numerals I-VIII in fig. 23.) They usually contained large mammoth bones, but lacked the dark layer of cultural debris on the bottom. They are all interpreted as caches--possibly for mammoth bone fuel.

In addition to the large peripheral pits, the upper surface of the dark lens was pockmarked by thirty smaller pits (1 m in diameter and 60-70 cm deep, on the average) and forty shallow depressions. Most of the sophisticated bone artifacts and art objects found at Avdeevo came from the smaller pits; they have therefore been interpreted as storage places for valuables. The depressions (covering up to several square meters) were frequently flanked by upright mammoth bones. They are regarded as work or activity areas, though the precise nature of the work associated with them remains unclear.

The entire feature complex of Avdeevo bears a striking resemblance to the equally remarkable complex found at Kostenki I-1 (fig. 24) (Klein 1969b:116-21). The only major difference is the absence of a string of hearths along the midline of the dark lens at Avdeevo (only one hearth was found; see fig. 23). One of the principal investigators of Avdeevo, A. N. Rogachev, has suggested (1953) that the hearths were obliterated by the same erosional processes that blurred the edges of many pits and depressions in the central part of the Avdeevo lens (unclear edges are signified by dotted lines in fig. 23).

The technical problems in roofing the huge areas of the Avdeevo and Kostenki I-1 feature complexes make it unlikely that each represents a single

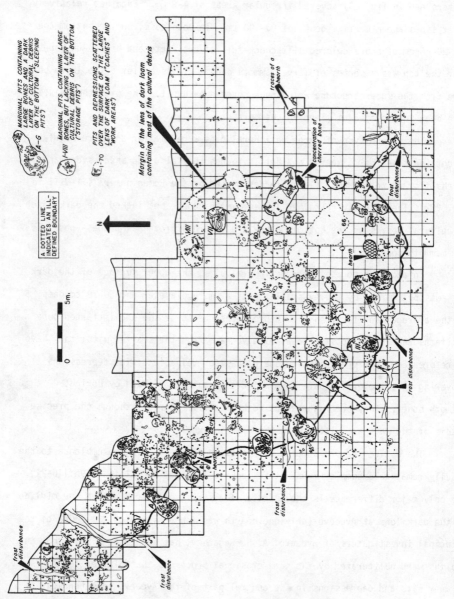

MARGINAL PITS CONTAINING
LARGE BONES AND A DARK
LAYER OF CULTURAL DEBRIS
ON THE BOTTOM ("SLEEPING
PITS")

MARGINAL PITS CONTAINING LARGE
BONES, BUT LACKING A LAYER OF
CULTURAL DEBRIS ON THE BOTTOM
("STORAGE PITS")

PITS AND DEPRESSIONS SCATTERED
OVER THE SURFACE OF THE LARGE
LENS OF DARK LOAM ("CACHES" AND
"WORK AREAS")

A DOTTED LINE
INDICATES AN ILL-
DEFINED BOUNDARY

N

0   5m.

Margin of the lens of dark loam
containing most of the cultural debris

traces of a
hearth

concentration of
charred bone

frost
disturbance

hearth

frost disturbance

frost
disturbance

hearth

frost
disturbance

frost
disturbance

Fig. 23.--Avdeevo. Plan of the excavations showing the principal features. (After Rogachev 1953, fig. 3.)

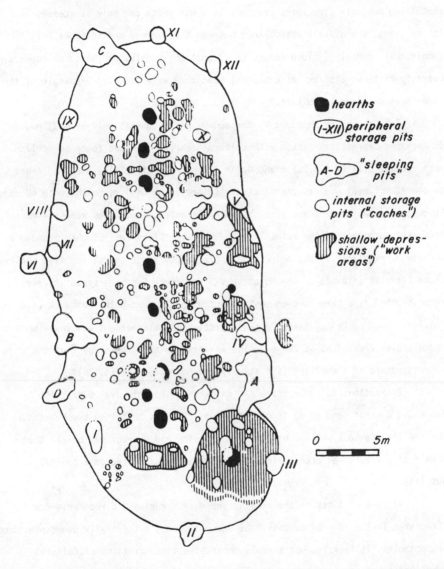

Fig. 24.--Kostenki I, horizon 1. Plan of the principal feature complex. (After Boriskovskij 1958, fig. 3.)

"long house," but exactly what is represented in each case remains uncertain. Most probably, in each instance, we are dealing with a complex settlement containing multiple structures arranged in a way which can only be guessed at. In any event, the overall resemblance between the Avdeevo and Kostenki I-1 complexes is certainly close enough to support the conclusion (based on the near identity of their artifact assemblages) that they were occupied by people of the same "Kostenki-Avdeevo culture."

The "ruins" in *Molodova V, horizons 7* and *6* consist only of shallow, dish-shaped depressions packed with cultural debris. The two found in horizon 7 were roughly oval (2.6 × 2.1 m and 4.0 × 1.6 m, respectively). The single one uncovered in level 6 approached a circle (diameter about 4 m, depth up to 40 cm). It contained two hearths and five possible postholes. Postholes were the most prominent component of the ruins in *Molodova V-3*. Sixty-four of them bounded a shallow, irregularly shaped depression containing a large hearth and five shallow cache (?) pits (fig. 25). The Molodova V-3 structure has been speculatively reconstructed as a skin-covered conical hut with a wooden-pole framework (fig. 25). Finally, *Molodova V-2* contained a concentration of reindeer antlers covering a roughly oval area of about 215 m^2. The antlers may have formed part of the superstructure of a dwelling (tentatively reconstructed in fig. 26).

Excavations in *Voronovitsa I-1* uncovered a roughly oval depression 2.5 × 3.8 m across and up to 35 cm deep (fig. 27). It contained two hearths, the smaller one in a shallow pit. The depression and hearths may be all that remain of a structure, once again imaginatively reconstructed as a conical hut (fig. 27).

At several sites in the Ukraine and nearby regions, direct evidence for structures in the form of mammoth bone accumulations, artificially dug depressions, or postholes, is lacking, but sharply demarcated concentrations of cultural debris nonetheless suggest that structures were present. Examples of such sites are *Grensk, horizon 2* (Bud'ko 1966:37-42), *Kajstrova Balka II* (Boriskovskij and Praslov 1964:29), and *Voronovitsa I, horizon 2* (Chernysh 1959:41-44).

Sometimes it is difficult to distinguish evidence for ancient buildings from postoccupational modification of a site by natural processes. Thus, at

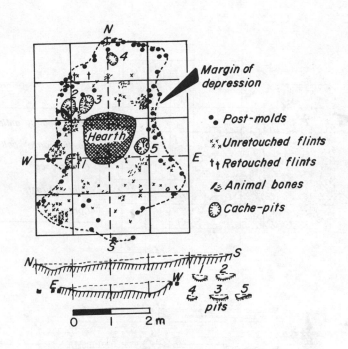

Fig. 25.--Molodova V, horizon 3. *Above*, plan and profiles of the base of an ancient structure; *below*, reconstruction of the ancient structure. (After Chernysh 1959, figs. 48, 49.)

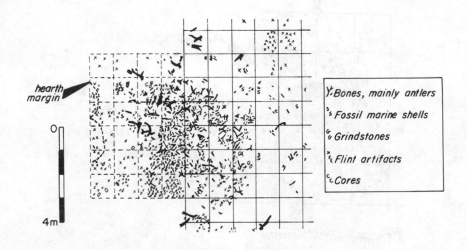

hearth
margin

0

4m

Y Bones, mainly antlers

s Fossil marine shells

G Grindstones

X Flint artifacts

c Cores

Fig. 26.--Molodova V, horizon 2. *Above*, concentration of reindeer antlers marking the location of an ancient structure; *below*, reconstruction of the dwelling. (After Chernysh 1959, fig. 51; 1961, fig. 43.)

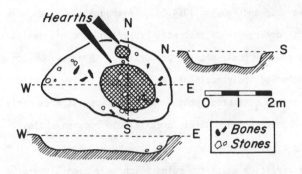

Fig. 27.--Voronovitsa I, horizon 1. *Above*, plan and profiles of the depressed foundation of an ancient structure; *below*, reconstruction of the structure. (After Chernysh 1959, figs. 20, 21.)

Osokorovka I and possibly at *Yamburg*, what were initially interpreted as postholes are now generally regarded as rodent burrows (Pidoplichko 1969:47), while at *Timonovka I*, intersecting ice-wedge casts were initially misinterpreted as evidence for large, rectangular, completely subterranean dwellings. The horizontal dimensions of these were estimated as 11.5-12 m × 3-3.5 m, with a depth of 2.5-3 m (Gorodtsov 1933, 1934, 1935a and b; also Efimenko 1953:546-47). The extraordinary earth-moving capabilities that the Timonovka ruins implied puzzled many archeologists until their natural origin was revealed (Velichko 1961b:156; Grekhova 1968). At *Amvrosievka*, a huge accumulation of bison bones, filling a gully 30 m long, 4-5 m wide, and more than 1 m deep, has sometimes been

interpreted as a structural remnant, but this possibility is now widely discounted (Boriskovskij and Praslov 1964:23). Although the bones were generally
not in anatomical order, few of them were broken-up, and all skeletal parts
were present in roughly their natural proportions. Nearly 1000 animals were
represented, including individuals of various ages. A few hundred artifacts
(both bone and stone) scattered amongst the bones suggest that early man played
a part in their accumulation, but his precise role remains unclear.

Even the brief descriptions which have been presented show that there
is considerable variation among the ruins which have been discovered at Upper
Paleolithic sites in the Ukraine and nearby areas. This variation may have
arisen in part as a result of the fact that people build different kinds of
structures, depending upon the season, the intended length of stay, and so forth.
But to a considerable extent it is probable that the variation is a further
reflection of the cultural diversity of the Ukrainian Upper Paleolithic. In
other words, in most cases the people who built the structures probably belonged
to different cultures in the narrow sense of the term.

There are many interesting questions about the Upper Paleolithic ruins
of the Ukraine (and elsewhere) which remain unanswered. For example, how many
people occupied the structures they represent and what was the duration of
occupation? Attempts to answer such questions are complicated by the absence of
hard data on the original dimensions and interior space of the structures (the
probability that any of the imaginative reconstructions are correct or even
nearly correct is difficult, if not impossible, to establish). In addition,
there are such important, unresolved problems as whether the multiple ruins of
sites like Avdeevo, Dobranichevka, and Mezin represent dwellings which were
occupied simultaneously or sequentially.

It is tempting to bring data on modern hunter-gatherers to bear on
questions of group size and duration of occupation, but this procedure is
extremely risky. Beyond the widely recognized caveat that the social and
cultural organization of many ethnographically known hunter-gatherers has been
profoundly affected by contact with more advanced peoples, and that it therefore
deviates from the aboriginal ("normal") condition, there is the far more

important point that most ethnographically studied hunter-gatherers have lived in marginal environments--environments, that is, in which plant and animal life are relatively meager and to which such hunter-gatherers have been progressively restricted by the development of more complex cultures, beginning in the early Holocene. And even in those few instances (for example, in the central valley of California or on the Pacific Northwest coast) where the resource base of ethnographically studied hunter-gatherers was fairly rich, the overall environment differed substantially from that faced by most, if not all, Upper Paleolithic peoples in middle latitude Europe. In fact, not since the Last Glacial has the earth possessed comparable environments in which an extremely adverse climate was combined with a relative abundance of big game. Many aspects of Upper Paleolithic sociocultural organization must have evolved in direct response to these peculiar environmental conditions and must have therefore been unique.

This is not to say that it is not fruitful to use observations on modern hunter-gatherers to reconstruct the life-ways of Pleistocene men (the next chapter makes quite explicit use of such observations), but simply that their use to estimate things like group size and duration of site occupation can never be more than suggestive. Turning back to the Ukraine, it seems best to attempt estimates which make no pretense of precision. At several sites the spectacular nature of the ruined dwellings, incorporating the bones of several dozen mammoths, suggests construction by many people, who would hardly have put forth the effort for an intended stay of only a few days. At many sites, including those with spectacular ruins, the presence of thousands of artifacts, including hundreds of seemingly finished implements, in combination with a great quantity of "kitchen debris" (broken-up bones), also indicates prolonged stay by more than just a few people. But whether a fairly prolonged stay is to be regarded as several weeks or several months or as often-repeated visits of several weeks or several months, remains unclear. Similarly, it is uncertain whether a group of "more than a few people" is to be considered as a few dozen or a few score. Probably the size of the cohabiting group varied from culture to culture and from season to season within a culture. Questions like these may never be satisfactorily resolved. At the very least, they remain problems for future research.

Disposal of the Dead at Ukrainian Last Glacial Sites

Although intentional burials have been found at both Mousterian and
Upper Paleolithic sites elsewhere (S. R. Binford, 1968b; Oakley et al. 1971),
none have been discovered at any of the principal sites discussed here. Only
a few isolated human skeletal fragments are known from these sites, and then
only from some of the Upper Paleolithic ones. These fragments are listed in
table 5. Although most of them are insufficient for taxonomic assessment, it
is assumed by analogy with more complete remains from Upper Paleolithic sites
elsewhere that they all came from anatomically modern men (*Homo sapiens sapiens*).
Similarly, by analogy with physical remains found in other areas, it is assumed
that the Mousterian inhabitants of the Ukraine and its environs were Neanderthals
(*Homo sapiens neanderthalensis*).

TABLE 5

HUMAN REMAINS FROM UPPER PALEOLITHIC SITES
IN THE UKRAINE AND NEARBY AREAS

Site	Remains	Basic Reference
Chulatovo I	Fragmentary left frontal and parietal of an adult	Boriskovskij 1953: 301-302
Eliseevichi	Clavicle, ribs, pelvis, femur, and other fragments of an infant's skeleton	Polikarpovich 1968: 168
Gorodok II	Fragments of an adult tibia and fibula and adult foot bones	Boriskovskij 1953: 145-47
Mezin	Crown of a lower right molar	Shovkoplyas 1965b: 104
Novgorod-Severskij	Humeral fragment and skull fragments of an adult	Boriskovskij 1953: 301-302
Pushkari I	Crown of an upper left deciduous molar	Boriskovskij 1953: 226
Yudinovo	Fragment of a right humerus	Polikarpovich 1968: 167
Korman IV	Fragment of a humerus	Botez 1933:430

SOURCE: After Klein et al. 1971.

Surveying the Mousterian and Upper Paleolithic burials known to her, S. R. Binford (1968b) found, among other things, that "grave goods" occurred in only about half (20/37) of the Mousterian examples, but in all (42) of the Upper Paleolithic ones. Generally speaking, she also found a tendency for more varied and elaborate burial rituals among Upper Paleolithic peoples, and the omissions from her sample that I am aware of--for example, the Upper Paleolithic burials at Kostenki on the Don (Klein 1969b) and at Sungir' northeast of Moscow (Bader 1965, 1970)--would further support this conclusion. In burial practices, as in other aspects of culture, Upper Paleolithic peoples seem to have been qualitatively distinct from Mousterians.

An interesting example of how data from burials can shed light on the culture of the living comes from the Upper Paleolithic site of Sungir', referred to in the last paragraph. Three of the burials found at this site were accompanied by strings of "beads" girdling the skeletons in a way that suggests they were sewn onto close-fitting clothing. This is even more direct evidence for Upper Paleolithic tailoring than the bone "needles" found at many sites.

One fact that should be emphasized is that burials in Mousterian and Upper Paleolithic sites are relatively rare occurrences, enough so that even a well-preserved Upper Paleolithic burial is able to command the attention of the popular press. The overwhelming majority of Mousterian and Upper Paleolithic sites have provided no burials. At best they contain, as do the sites listed in table 5, an odd scrap or two of human bone. Several explanations of this are possible. On the one hand, it is possible that Last Glacial peoples did not usually bury their dead in, at, or near their occupation sites. Alternatively, it is conceivable that many Last Glacial peoples did not bury their dead at all, but disposed of them by cremation or other equally destructive means. It is also possible that, subsequent to burial, graves were frequently disrupted by scavengers. Certainly the permanently frozen subsoil that covered much of the European USSR throughout the Last Glacial would have made it difficult to dig deep, well-protected graves. Scavenger-disturbance of shallow graves may in fact account for most of the isolated human remains listed in table 5.

Conclusions

Information which has been presented in this chapter suggests that both Mousterian and Upper Paleolithic peoples had successfully adapted to the harsh environments which existed in the Ukraine during the Last Glacial. Both peoples met the challenge of extraordinary cold by incorporating significant quantities of high-energy food (meat) in their diets, by building substantial, heated dwellings, and probably also by manufacturing clothing (reasonably documented at least for the Upper Paleolithic). Various evidence (especially a greater number of sites) suggests that the adaptations achieved by Upper Paleolithic Ukrainians were superior to those of the Mousterians. This point will be further elaborated in the next chapter.

Readers who are familiar with the widely publicized French Upper Paleolithic succession, with its possibly contemporaneous Aurignacian and Périgoridian cultures, followed first by the Solutrean and then by the Magdalenian, may wonder why the Ukrainian Upper Paleolithic sites cannot be grouped into an equally simple sequence of successive cultures. It must be noted to begin with, however, that detailed and comprehensive treatments of the French succession, especially in its heartland of southwest France (de Sonneville-Bordes 1960), clearly show that it was far more complex than the conventional 3- to 4-stage scheme, and some investigators (for example, Movius 1966:297) have hinted that even the most comprehensive treatments may not do justice to the complexity that actually existed. The total number of distinctive Upper Paleolithic cultures present in France is a matter for ongoing debate, but it was certainly far more than the three or four which are simplistically listed in most elementary (and some not-so-elementary) texts.

It is important to realize, moreover, that the Upper Paleolithic sites of the Ukraine and nearby regions are scattered over an area significantly larger than France.[4] In fact, given the marked variability in time and space which is

---

4. The contrast in size between the Ukraine and the Upper Paleolithic heartland of southwest France is, of course, even greater.

a characteristic of the Upper Paleolithic wherever it has been found, its 25,000 year time-span (from roughly 35,000 to 10,000 B.P.), the vast area of the Ukraine, and the relatively small number of known Ukrainian Upper Paleolithic sites (at most 60 versus more than 150 for southwest France), it would be remarkable indeed if the Ukrainian sites could be lumped into a very small number of cultures.

5. SOME CONCLUSIONS AND SPECULATIONS ON THE
MOUSTERIAN AND THE UPPER PALEOLITHIC

The Problem of "Transitional Cultures"

Sometime between 45,000 and 35,000 years ago (the exact time perhaps
depending upon the place), the Mousterian culture complex was rather abruptly
supplanted in the Ukraine and in other parts of its range by the Upper Paleolithic block of cultures. Although human skeletal remains have not yet been
found at Mousterian sites in the Ukraine and are extremely rare at Upper Paleolithic sites there, sufficient evidence is available from other areas to suggest
that the demise of the Mousterian and the appearance of the Upper Paleolithic
was intimately connected with the disappearance of Neanderthal man (*Homo sapiens
neanderthalensis*) and the advent of modern man (*Homo sapiens sapiens*).

For many years, students of early man have disagreed as to whether
modern man evolved over a broad front in many related Neanderthal populations or
originated in a fairly limited area and dispersed from there. Similarly, there
has been debate over whether the Upper Paleolithic developed repeatedly from
different local Mousterian cultures or spread from a single more or less
restricted birthplace, diversifying afterwards. With the possible exception of
Radomyshl' in the Dnepr basin (Shovkoplyas 1965a), which has been inadequately
documented and where it is possible that excavation mixed Upper Paleolithic and
Mousterian occupation horizons, the European USSR (including the Ukraine)
contains no site about which it could be argued that there is evidence for the
Mousterian evolving into the Upper Paleolithic. The most vigorous arguments for
the evolution of a local Mousterian into a local Upper Paleolithic have been

114

made for other areas--especially France (Bordes 1958; 1968a:147-52), Hungary
(Vértes 1965b; Valoch 1968:358; Gábori 1969), and the Levant (Garrod 1951, 1955;
cf. Copeland 1970). These arguments are based on the presence in each area of a
stone-tool "culture" which is supposed to be chronologically and typologically
intermediate between the Mousterian and the Upper Paleolithic. Implicit in
these arguments is the assumption that gross similarities between two chronologically successive stone-tool cultures indicate a genetic (parent-offspring)
relationship analogous to the ones that have been suggested for many similar and
chronologically successive fossil organisms. Stone tools, however, are not
organisms, and more particularly, to paraphrase S. R. Binford (1968c:708), they
do not have the capacity to mutate, breed, and evolve as organisms do.[1] The
whole concept of transitional cultures analogous to "missing links" in the fossil
record is therefore open to question.

Frameworks for the interpretation of similarities and differences among
stone artifact assemblages in culturally meaningful (superorganic) terms are only
now being developed (by L. R. Binford, S. R. Binford, L. G. Freeman, H. L. Movius,
and J. R. Sackett, to name just those whose work has been previously cited).
For the moment the possible significance of so-called transitional cultures is a
matter for open speculation. An interpretation (speculation) which is at least
as plausible as the missing-link hypothesis is that the transitional cultures
reflect diffusion of Upper Paleolithic traits into a Mousterian context. This
interpretation can be illustrated with facts on the French "transitional culture,"
the Périgordian I or Châtelperronian. Although the mixture of Mousterian and
Upper Paleolithic elements in this "culture" is not open to dispute, its hypothetical ancestry to the later or Upper Périgordian series of cultures (Bordes
1968b) can be and has been questioned (see, for example, Cheynier 1963: Lynch
1966:182-87; or Clark 1967:53). The most serious objection is the theoretical
one which has been voiced here--namely, that gross similarities between temporally
successive artifact assemblages do not necessarily imply historical continuity

---

1. This point was clearly made in 1949 by H. L. Movius, Jr., in specific
reference to the archeology of early man in the Old World, but it has only been
recently that a significant number of investigators have seriously considered its
implications.

between them. In any case, it is widely agreed that whatever descended from the Périgordian I, it was not the early Aurignacian, which was apparently intrusive into France and which was in fact the earliest full-blown Upper Paleolithic there. The time and place of the origin of the Aurignacian need not concern us,[2] but it is important that it seems to have overlapped in time the Périgordian I. This is suggested by stratigraphic intercalation of Périgordian I and early Aurignacian horizons at le Piage and Roc de Combe (Bordes 1968b:60-61), and less directly by C-14 dates such as 33,860 ± 250 (GrN-1742) on the Périgordian I of the Grotte du Renne (Vogel and Waterbolk 1963) and 33,300 ± 760 (GrN-4610), 33,330 ± 410 (GrN-4720), and 34,250 ± 675 (GrN-4507) on the early Aurignacian of the Abri Pataud (Vogel and Waterbolk 1967). The early Aurignacian was thus in the right place at the right time to provide a diffusionary source of traits to the Périgordian I.

It may be objected that if the early Aurignacian were the source of Upper Paleolithic elements in the Périgordian I, these elements would be more Aurignacian-like, which admittedly they are not. But this objection may be countered by the ethnographic observation that often what is diffused is not a precise blueprint, but an imperfectly understood or subsequently modified idea of how to do something. The implication here is that we cannot rule out historical connections between artifact assemblages because they lack detailed similarities any more than we can assert a definite link between them because they are roughly similar. Contrary to the conclusions that have been reached using organic models for the interpretation of similarities and differences among artifact assemblages, it is therefore possible that the historical relationships of the Périgordian I were with the Aurignacian and not the later Périgordian.

The fate of the Périgordian I may have been "extinction without issue." The available evidence suggests it was rather abruptly supplanted by the early Aurignacian, though perhaps not at the same time everywhere.[3] The theoretical

---

2. The available evidence suggests a southeast European-southwest Asian origin prior to 40,000 years ago (see below).

3. The Périgordian I-early Aurignacian interface is hard to date with precision because it falls in a time interval (more than 30,000 years ago) for which it is difficult to obtain true ages by the radiocarbon method. See the next section.

difficulty in establishing a historical ("genetic") link between the Périgordian I and the later so-called Périgordian developments has already been discussed.

The varying nature and, possibly, duration of the culture-contact situation in different parts of France may be responsible for the striking variability that Bordes (1968b:62) has noted within the Périgordian I. At the very least, a reader who is skeptical of the culture-contact hypothesis--and it is admittedly only speculative--should read the separate accounts of the Péri- gordian I occurrences and especially of the truly remarkable Périgordian I of the Grotte du Renne (Leroi-Gourhan 1965; Movius 1969). He will certainly be struck by the complexity of the Périgordian I problem and impressed by the impossibility of formulating a simple, straightforward solution.[4] The other instances of supposedly transitional cultures are at least as complicated and as far from final solution.

It would certainly be interesting to know what the people who made Péri- gordian I artifacts looked like--whether they were Neanderthals in the narrow sense, anatomically modern men, or something in between. A very modern-looking skeleton found at the Roc de Combe-Capelle in 1909 has often been attributed to a Périgordian I layer there (de Sonneville-Bordes 1959:20-23), but its precise stratigraphic provenience and indeed the stratigraphy of the site remain open to question (Lynch 1966:165-69). The only securely documented human remains from a Périgordian I occurrence are a series of teeth from the Grotte du Renne (Leroi- Gourhan 1958). Although they are said to be rather archaic looking, they are in- sufficient in themselves to establish the overall appearance of their former owners. As C. L. Brace (1966:37) has pointed out, the teeth of the well-known Italian Upper Paleolithic, possibly Aurignacian, Grimaldi "youth" are also rather archaic looking, yet the total morphological pattern of the Grimaldi remains is undeniably modern. The lack of more complete, well-documented human remains

---

4. A further complication in attempting to understand the Périgordian I has been called to my attention by C. G. Sampson. This is the interesting Périgordian I-like occurrence which has been well-documented by A. Palma di Cesnola (1966) from the Grotta del Cavallo in the heel of the Italian boot. Located far from the nearest French Périgordian I sites, the Grotta del Cavallo Périgordian I-like assemblages have been dubbed "Uluzzian" by Palma di Cesnola (after nearby Uluzzo Bay). They are dated to "greater than 31,000 B.P." (Alessio et al. 1970: 603-4).

from "transitional cultures" in Europe is a major gap in the data on the nature of the "passage" from the Mousterian to the Upper Paleolithic.

The Relevance of Radiocarbon Dates
and Physical Remains

It would seem, from the radiocarbon dates cited in the previous discussion and from other, general considerations, that the radiocarbon method ought to be an important tool in understanding the Mousterian-Upper Paleolithic interface. Thus, the hypothesis that the Upper Paleolithic originated in just one area and spread from there would certainly be supported by dating evidence that the Upper Paleolithic appeared later in areas further from its supposed birthplace. Conversely, the multiple evolution of Mousterian cultures into Upper Paleolithic ones would presumably find support in a completely random geographic scatter of late Mousterian-early Upper Paleolithic dates. Unfortunately, however, the time interval with which we are dealing (45,000-35,000 B.P.) is one for which it is difficult to obtain totally satisfactory C-14 dates. The major problem is that after this much time has passed, so little original C-14 is left in a sample that even a minute amount of recent carbon contamination will make the sample much "too young." For instance, a sample that is actually 37,000 years old will retain only 1 percent of its original C-14. At the same time, an addition of only 1 percent recent (for example, humic or rootlet) carbon contaminant will give the sample an apparent age of about 31,000 years (Vogel 1966). And even in the best laboratories, it is difficult to be certain that pretreatment has removed the very small amounts of contaminant that could lead to serious age distortion. For this reason, many conservative scholars prefer to look upon all dates in excess of 30,000 to 40,000 years as no more than minimum (stated age or older) dates.

Since contamination by recent carbon and resultant distortion in the direction of "too young" is the major problem, it is obviously more relevant to search for patterning in the oldest Upper Paleolithic dates than in the youngest Mousterian ones. Until recently it could be argued that there were too few dates to establish statistically significant patterning, but this no longer seems to be the case. While there are no dates on the Upper Paleolithic of western

Europe older than about 35,000 B.P. (see Vogel 1966; Vogel and Waterbolk 1967;

and recent issues of *Radiocarbon*), there is now little doubt that the Upper

Paleolithic of eastern and southeastern Europe is older than this. This is

shown by the dates of 44,300 ± 1,900 (GrN-4659) and 39,700 ± 900 (GrN-4658) on

successive early Aurignacian levels at Istállóskö Cave (Hungary), 35,200 ± 670

(GrN-4590) on the early Aurignacian of Peskö Cave (Hungary), 42,700 ± 127

(GrN-5181) on the possibly Aurignacian of Samuilica Cave (Bulgaria) (all cited

dates from Vogel and Waterbolk 1972), and less certainly by > 41,700 (GX-0197)

(Gábori-Cjánk 1970) and 43,000 ± 1,100 (GrN-6058) (Vogel and Waterbolk 1972) on

the transitional "early Szeletian culture" of Szeleta Cave (Hungary), > 37,700

(GX-0198) (Gábori-Cjánk 1970) on the possibly early Szeletian of Büdöspesht Cave

(Hungary), 38,500 ± 1,250 (GrN-2181) (Chmielewski 1965) on the transitional

"Jerzmanowice culture" of Nietoperzowa Cave (Poland), and 38,400 + 2,800 or

- 2,100 (GrN-2438) (Valoch 1969) on the transitional "Szeletian" of Čertova pec

(Czechoslovakia). It is also pertinent to point out that a series of acceptable

dates from the Haua Fteah and Ed Dabba caves in Cyrenaican Libya indicate that

the Mousterian-Upper Paleolithic interface there is at least 38,000 years old

(Vogel and Waterbolk 1963; Smith 1965; Vogel 1966), and a comparable or older

age is possible for the earliest Upper Paleolithic of Iraq.[5]

Since the Ukraine shares a border with Hungary, it may also eventually

provide Upper Paleolithic sites older than any in western Europe. In fact,

it may already contain some in levels 9 and 10 of Molodova V. It is entirely

possible that the available C-14 dates on these levels--in the 28,000-29,000

year range (see table 2)--are much too young. A true age of as much as 40,000

years is suggested by their stratification within a complex suite of middle

---

5. C-14 dates in the 35,000 year range are available on the base of
the early Aurignacian (Baradostian) occupation at the important Iraqi site of
Shanidar Cave (Vogel and Waterbolk 1963; Solecki 1963, 1971). The top of the
underlying Mousterian is dated to at least 46,000 B.P., leaving a 10,000 year
hiatus during which the local Upper Paleolithic may have appeared.

Würm sediments (chap. 2).[6]

Admitting that it is not yet possible to deal conclusively with such puzzling phenomena as the Périgordian I, it nonetheless seems to me that the radiocarbon data may be used as a strong argument in favor of a restricted origin for the Upper Paleolithic in eastern-southeastern Europe or perhaps in nearby southwest Asia (the Near East) or both. Southwest Asia must be considered not only because of what may be the very early appearance of the Upper Paleolithic at Shanidar in Iraq and in nearby Libya, but also because it has provided relevant and fairly abundant human remains. These remains may be interpreted to suggest that an earlier, "near-classic" variety of Neanderthals (for example, at Shanidar and at Amud Cave and Tabūn in Israel) evolved into modern or near-modern men (for example, at Skhūl and Qafzeh in Israel) during the course of the Mousterian (Howell 1965:chap. 6; also 1957; Vandermeersch 1969). Further, S. R. Binford (1968c, 1970) has detected evidence for a shift within the Mousterian of the Levant from a generalized hunting pattern (earlier) to the specialized hunting of just one or two species (later). The specialized pattern is the one she claims for the subsequent Upper Paleolithic in the Near East and elsewhere.[7]

The human fossil record of eastern-southeastern Europe may also contain evidence for the appearance of modern or near-modern man before the end of the Mousterian, but the data there are still too scanty and insecure to make a truly

---

6. It is noteworthy that the Groningen laboratory in the Netherlands, which has supplied all the most relevant dates on the earliest Upper Paleolithic, has recently dated samples from the Russian Upper Paleolithic site of Sungir' to 25,500 ± 200 (GrN-5425) and 24,430 ± 400 (GrN-5446) (Vogel and Waterbolk 1972). These dates are significantly older than those obtained on Sungir' in the Soviet Union. The Soviet Sungir' determinations are 14,600 ± 600 (GIN-14) (Cherdyntsev et al. 1964) and 21,800 ± 1,000 (GIN-326a) and 22,500 ± 600 (GIN-326b) (Cherdyntsev et al. 1969). This kind of discrepancy between laboratories presumably reflects differences in sample preparation procedures and could be expected to grow as the true age of a sample increased. This means that Groningen determinations of Molodova V-9, 10 samples might well come out several thousand years older than the present dates.

7. I am not actually sure that wide-spectrum hunting versus concentration on just one or two species could be demonstrated to differentiate the Mousterian from the Upper Paleolithic in most parts of Europe, though the fault may lie in the absence of species-frequency information for many sites. Binford's hypothesis, however, is an interesting one which certainly demands serious testing.

persuasive argument. In western Europe, however, where the fossil record is comparatively rich, no obvious trend toward modern man within the Mousterian is apparent. On the contrary, Howell (1965:chap. 6) has argued that the Neander- thals of western Europe became more, rather than less, "classic" as time passed. This in turn makes it seem exceedingly unlikely that they evolved independently into modern man.[8] One point that deserves special emphasis is that if modern man originated in southeastern Europe-southwest Asia and dispersed from there, he need not have physically exterminated his more archaic-looking contemporaries. Belonging to the same species, he could have interbred with them, and if, as the archeological record suggests, he was many times more numerous, the frequencies of "archaic genes" would have been very low in the gene pools of hybrid popula- tions. Archaic morphological features would have become correspondingly rare. In sum, the process of replacement could have been as much or more by genetic swamping than by physical destruction.

To this point, discussion has proceeded as if areas of the world other than Europe, southwest Asia, and North Africa were known to be irrelevant to the question of modern human origins. In fact, quite the reverse is true. Remarkably little is known about human physical and cultural evolution in the late Pleisto- cene of southern Asia and sub-Saharan Africa. Indeed, recent discoveries of very modern looking physical remains in quite old contexts in Borneo (Brothwell 1960) and Ethiopia (Leakey, Butzer, and Day 1969) suggest that these areas may be far from irrelevant. Accordingly, it is entirely possible that the hypothesis advanced here may require serious modification in the future.

The Nature of the Contrast

Whether it is ultimately proven that the Upper Paleolithic was intrusive in most places or that it originated locally again and again, it seems reasonable to argue that the way of life of Upper Paleolithic peoples in the Ukraine and elsewhere in Europe was very different from that of the Mousterians. Unlike the

---

8. For an overall perspective on this, however, the reader should review the opposing arguments of Brace (1964, 1967: chap. 12).

Mousterians, Upper Paleolithic peoples tended to make most of their tools on blades. They made an even greater variety of stone tools than did the Mousterians and emphasized various types of end-scrapers and burins as opposed to side-scrapers and points. Sometimes they seem to have transported or imported high-quality or luxury raw materials over distances of hundreds of kilometers, while there is no evidence in the Mousterian for such a phenomenon. In contrast to the Mousterians, who worked bone only on occasion, Upper Paleolithic peoples worked it in profusion, turning out a wide variety of bone artifacts. Often they transformed bone, antler, ivory, and other materials into clearly recognizable art objects. Undoubted art objects or ornaments are entirely absent in the Mousterian. The distribution of the Upper Paleolithic also suggests a qualitative difference from the Mousterian, for while the site of Khotylevo at 54°N constitutes the northernmost Mousterian site known, Upper Paleolithic sites have been found on the Arctic Circle.[9] Finally, Upper Paleolithic people seem to have been much more numerous than their Mousterian predecessors. This is shown by the fact that their sites are many times more abundant than Mousterian sites, while there is no evidence to suggest that, on the average, individual Upper Paleolithic sites were occupied for shorter periods than were Mousterian ones. If anything, Upper Paleolithic peoples were less nomadic than the Mousterians, since Upper Paleolithic sites very frequently contain remains of what seem to have been semipermanent structures.

In the long-term view of culture history, the Upper Paleolithic appears to constitute a quantum advance over the Mousterian. This advance was probably manifest not only in material culture and technology, which have been

---

9. The most striking example is the site of Byzovaya at 65° N on the Pechora River just west of the northern Urals. This remarkable site, dated by a single unconfirmed C-14 determination of 18,320 ± 280 (TA-121), contained several dozen artifacts and bones of no less than twenty-one mammoths, three reindeer, seven wolves, one horse, and one rhinoceros (Bader 1969a). It is only one of several interesting Upper Paleolithic localities which have been found in the northern Urals in recent years (Bader 1969a, b). A report that one of these (Krutaya gora) has also provided in situ Mousterian artifacts (Chard 1969:776; Bader 1969a) must be discounted, however. The geological context of the supposed Mousterian artifacts indicates a very late Pleistocene, possibly late Würm age (Ivanova 1969d:25-26), and it is possible that they derive from an outlier of the "Siberian Upper Paleolithic," which in some ways is superficially more like the Mousterian than the European Upper Paleolithic (Klein 1971).

emphasized so far, but also in social organization. Unfortunately, social
organization does not fossilize in the same way or to the same extent as does
technology, and it is necessary to make extensive use of ethnographic analogy
in reconstructing it. One major limitation on the use of modern analogy to
reconstruct Last Glacial life-ways in Europe--the lack of environmental compara-
bility--was discussed in the previous chapter, and it must be added here that
data on modern peoples may have especially limited application to the Mousterians.
Their physical characteristics, in combination with such cultural facts as the
absence of undoubted art objects in Mousterian sites, suggest they *may* have been
"primitives" in the narrowest imaginable sense of that word. Thus, in addition
to possessing simpler cultures than we do, they may also have been biopsychologically less complex.[10] Putting it another way, if an ethnographer were suddenly
to be presented with a living Mousterian group, he might well find that his
traditional descriptive categories (kinship, economy, religion, communication,
and so forth) would still be applicable, but not in the same fashion as they are
to modern primitives or for that matter to any modern peoples. With regard to
communication, for example, he would probably find that Neanderthals had
language, but whether their language could be described and analyzed by procedures
worked out in linguistics to treat modern languages is highly questionable.
It is entirely possible that Neanderthal language was truly primitive, a devel-
opmental stage before the acquisition of language as modern linguists know it.
This example can be carried no further, however, because archeological evidence
for the specific features of Neanderthal communication systems is nonexistent.

If for heuristic purposes we put aside the very important proviso
concerning the possible biopsychological distinctiveness of Mousterians, we can
attempt to use observations on modern peoples with a similar subsistence base
to reconstruct some important aspects of Mousterian social organization. The
archeological data indicate clearly that the Mousterians were hunter-gatherers.
Most modern peoples who hunt and gather for a living are organized at what has
been called the "band level of sociocultural integration" (Service 1966, 1971:

---

10. Modern so-called primitives differ from other modern peoples only in
the relative complexity of their cultures, not in their biopsychological makeup.

chap. 3). They live in relatively small groups (usually between 30 and 100 individuals) which roam over a reasonably well-defined territory in search of food and other vital items. Movement over the territory is not random, but is directed by seasonal and other factors determining the distribution of resources. Band societies are generally exogamous--that is, marriage is prohibited within one's own band, and mates must be sought in neighboring groups. This sort of arrangement helps to ensure that relations between nearby bands will be reasonably cordial--an obvious advantage when, for example, one's own territory is temporarily depleted of food and it is necessary to move for a while onto the territory of a neighbor.

Internally, bands are relatively unstructured societies, sex and age constituting the most important role-differentiating criteria. Younger men are usually charged with hunting, while women take primary responsibility for child-rearing and also for gathering whatever resources (mainly plant foods) that occur near the base camp.[11] Older men who can no longer hunt stay at the home base with the women and children. They are highly valued for the advice they can give younger people on the likely whereabouts of game, on the proper way to conduct ceremonies, and on other matters of general import. Leadership in band society tends to be achieved--that is, a good hunter or wise old man will be followed in his own sphere regardless of what his parentage may have been. In economic terms, band societies are characterized internally by the pooling and sharing of resources, and there are no important long-term differences in wealth among individuals or families. Sharing helps to make for fairly cordial relations within bands and thus promotes the survival of the band as a whole.

Like their Mousterian predecessors, many of the Upper Paleolithic peoples of Europe may also have been organized into bands. But the rather impressive *features* found at many sites and the sheer number of sites in some areas, indicating occupation by relatively large populations with a highly

---

11. The gathered component of the diet is actually larger by bulk than the hunted component in most hunter-gatherer societies, but this was probably not the case among many Last Glacial peoples in Europe.

effective big-game hunting technology, suggest that at least some Upper Paleolithic peoples may have been organized at the somewhat higher level of sociocultural
complexity known as the tribe (Service 1971: chap.4; Sahlins 1968). In many
respects, tribes are similar to bands. Basically, for example, they are egali-
tarian societies in which status is achieved rather than ascribed. Residential
groups at the tribal level need be no larger than bands (that is, 30 to 100 people),
but neighboring groups are characterized by far closer relationships than exist
among bands. These relationships are maintained and reinforced by the development
of pantribal institutions such as dispersed clans, age grades, or secret societies. Individuals belonging to a single clan or age grade will be spread throughout the tribe--that is, each band size unit will have some members representing
the same clans or age grades. Thus,at least for some purposes, for example, rit-
ual or ceremonial ones, a person in any given band-sized group will feel closer
to individuals in other groups than to persons in his own group. This makes for
closer relationships among groups than was possible at the band level.

It is easy to imagine how closer relationships among groups would have
allowed more successful cultural adaptations to the environmental circumstances
of the Last Glacial in Europe. Many, if not most,of the great herbivores that
Last Glacial peoples hunted were probably differentially distributed with the
seasons of the year. Some species may have grazed on the open interfluves
in summer, moving into the sheltered valleys in winter. Others may have migrated
north in spring and south in fall, using the natural routes provided by the great
river valleys. In any case, by analogy with modern gregarious herbivores, it is
probable that there were great seasonal concentrations of animals alternating
with periods of relative dispersal. Under these circumstances, the animals
would have been most effectively exploited by human groups that could also
periodically coalesce and disperse. Pantribal institutions would have facilitated
not only coalescence, but also the cooperative methods that were probably the
most effective means of hunting the large herbivores. More effective hunting
would in turn have promoted population growth. And it may not be irrelevant
that the ability to forge relatively large groups, at least temporarily, would
have given tribesmen a numerical advantage in any physical struggle with more

simply organized peoples.

In fact, it could even be argued that the development of pantribal institutions (and thus of the tribe) was one of the basic factors that led to the evolutionary success of the Upper Paleolithic over the Mousterian (cf. S. R. Binford 1970). The full process may actually have been a very complicated one involving interaction among a large series of variables of which greater social complexity was only one. Other variables that may have been important were advances in communication (language)[12] and in the ability to analyze the habits of game. These last two factors may in turn have been related to biological evolution in intellectual capacity (brain structure). Increased intellectual capacity could moreover have been both a cause and an effect of greater social complexity. In short, the appearance of modern man and the Upper Paleolithic may well have come about as the result of complex feedback among a number of biological, cultural, and environmental variables. Whatever the answer, no one can fail to be fascinated by the problem.

---

12. Research by Marshack (1972 and elsewhere) on the engraved patterns and designs frequently found on Upper Paleolithic bone objects has shown that they are far more complex than was hitherto thought. They may in fact constitute evidence for the completely modern sort of language. No such evidence is available from the Mousterian. Marshack's work generally supports the implication that Upper Paleolithic peoples were the intellectual equals of living man.

REFERENCES

Abbreviations

AN   Akademiya Nauk [Academy of sciences]

AO (year) g. *Arkheologicheskie otkrytiya* ____ *goda* [Archeological discoveries of (year)]. Moscow: Nauka, various years

BKICP   *Byulleten' Komissii po izucheniyu chetvertichnogo perioda* [Bulletin of the Commission for the Study of the Quaternary Period]

BMOIP   *Byulleten' Moskovskogo obshchestva ispytatelej prirody* [Bulletin of the Moscow Natural History Society]

KSIA   *Kratkie soobshcheniya Instituta arkheologii* [Brief communications of the Institute of Archeology]

KSIIMK   *Kratkie soobshcheniya Instituta istorii material'noj kul'tury* [Brief communications of the Institute of the History of Material Culture]

LPPNTSVE   *Less-periglyatsial-paleolit na territorii Srednej i Vostochnoj Evropy* [Loess-Periglacial-Paleolithic on the territory of central and eastern Europe]. Moscow, 1969

MIA   *Materialy i issledovaniya po arkheologii SSSR* [Materials and Investigations on the archaeology of the USSR]

MVSPICP   *Materialy vsesoyuznogo soveshchaniya po izucheniyu chetvertichnogo perioda* [Materials of the All-Union Conference on the Study of the Quaternary Period]. Moscow, 1961.

PIRPO   *Priroda i razvitie pervobytnogo obshchestva* [Environment and the development of primitive society] Moscow: Nauka, 1969

SA   *Sovetskaya arkheologiya* [Soviet archaeology]

SE   *Sovetskaya etnografiya* [Soviet ethnography]

SPPVTE   *Stratigrafiya i periodizatsiya paleolita Vostochnoj i Tsentral'noj Evropy* [Stratigraphy and periodization of the Paleolithic of eastern and central Europe] Moscow: Nauka, 1965

TKICP   *Trudy Komissii po izucheniyu chetvertichnogo perioda* [Transactions of the Commission for the Study of the Quaternary Period]

ABRAMOVA, Z. A. 1962. *Paleolithic art in the territory of the USSR* (in Russian). Moscow and Leningrad: AN SSSR.

ABRAMOVA, Z. A. 1966. *Depictions of man in the Paleolithic art of Eurasia* (in Russian). Moscow and Leningrad: Nauka.

ALEKSANDROVA, L. P., et al. 1971. Mammals (in Russian). In *Plejstotsen Tiraspolya,* pp. 70-170. Kishinev: Shtiintsa.

ALEKSEEV, V. A.; IVANOVA, I. K.; KIND, N. V.; and CHERNYSH, A. P. 1964. New data on the determination of the absolute age of the Upper Paleolithic levels of the site of Molodova V on the Middle Dnestr (in Russian). *Doklady AN SSSR* 156, no. 2:315-17.

ALESSIO, M.; BELLA, F.; IMPROTA, S.; BELLUOMINI, G.; TORESI, C.; and TURI, B. 1970. University of Rome radiocarbon dates VIII. *Radiocarbon* 12, no. 2: 599-616.

AMBROZEWICZ, C. 1930. Beiträge zur Kenntnis der Aurignacien-kultur Bessarabiens und der Bukowina. *Weiner Prähistorische Zeitschrift* 17:17-45.

ANISYUTKIN, N.K. 1969. The Mousterian site of Stinka on the middle Dnestr (in Russian). *Arkheologicheskij Sbornik* 11:5-17.

ANISYUTKIN, N. K. 1970. Investigation of Mousterian sites in Chernovtsy *oblast'* (in Russian). *AO 1969 g.,* pp. 219-20.

BADER, O. N. 1965. The most ancient Upper Paleolithic burials near Sungir' (in Russian). *Vestnik AN SSSR,* no. 5, pp. 77-80.

BADER, O. N. 1969a. A field seminar on the Anthropogene stratigraphy and Paleolithic of the Pechora subpolar region in 1968 (in Russian). *SA,* no. 4, pp. 305-10.

BADER, O. N. 1969b. The northern Paleolithic expedition (in Russian). *AO 1968 g.,* pp. 145-46.

BADER, O. N. 1970. The second Paleolithic grave at Sungir' (in Russian). *AO 1969 g.,* pp. 41-43.

BANDY, O. I.; BUTLER, E. A.; and WRIGHT, R. C. 1969. Alaskan Upper Miocene glacial deposits and the *Tuberotalia pachyderma* datum plane. *Science* 166:607-9.

BEREGOVAYA, N. A. 1960. Paleolithic localities of the USSR (in Russian). *MIA,* no. 81.

BERG, L. S. 1950. *Natural regions of the USSR.* Translated from the Russian by Olga Adler Titelbaum. New York: Macmillan.

BINFORD, L. R., and BINFORD, S. R. 1966. A preliminary analysis of functional variability in the Mousterian of Levallois facies. *American Anthropologist* 68 (no. 2, pt. 2):238-95.

BINFORD, S. R. 1968a. Variability and change in the near eastern Mousterian of Levallois facies. In *New perspectives in archeology,* ed. S. R. Binford and L. R. Binford, pp. 49-60. Chicago: Aldine.

BINFORD, S. R. 1968b. A structural comparison of disposal of the dead in the Mousterian and Upper Paleolithic. *Southwestern Journal of Anthropology* 24:139-54.

BINFORD, S. R. 1968c. Early Upper Pleistocene adaptations in the Levant. *American Anthropologist* 70, no. 4:707-17.

BINFORD, S. R. 1970. Late middle Paleolithic adaptations in the Levant and their possible consequences. *BioScience* 20:280-83.

BINFORD, S. R., and BINFORD, L. R. 1969. Stone tools and human behavior. *Scientific American* 220, no. 4:70-84.

BISHOP, W. W. 1971. The late Cenozoic history of east Africa in relation to hominoid evolution. In *Late Cenozoic glacial ages*, ed. K. K. Turekian, pp. 493-527. New Haven: Yale University Press.

BLOOM, A. L. 1971. Glacial-eustatic and isostatic controls of sea level since the Last Glaciation. In *Late Cenozoic glacial ages*, ed. K. K. Turekian, pp. 355-80. New Haven: Yale University Press.

BOBRINSKIJ, N. A.; KUZNETSOV, B. A., and KUZYAKIN, A. P. 1965. *Index of Mammals of the USSR* (in Russian). Moscow: Nauka.

BORDES, F. H. 1947. Etude comparative des différentes techniques de taille du silex et des roches dures. *L'Anthropologie* 51:1-29.

BORDES, F. H. 1958. Le passage du Paléolithique moyen au Paléolithique supérieur. In *Neanderthal Centenary*, ed. G. von Koenigswald, pp. 175-81. Utrecht: Kemink en Zoon.

BORDES, F. H. 1961a. Typologie du Paléolithique moyen et ancien. Bordeaux, Publications de l'Institut de Préhistoire de l'Université de Bordeaux, memoire no. 1.

BORDES, F. H. 1961b. Mousterian cultures in France. *Science* 134:803-10.

BORDES, F. H. 1968a. *The Old Stone Age*. New York: McGraw-Hill.

BORDES, F. H. 1968b. La question périgordienne. In *La Préhistoire: Problèmes et Tendances*, pp. 59-70. Paris: Centre National de la Recherche Scientifique.

BORDES, F. H. 1972. *A tale of two caves*. New York: Harper and Row.

BORISKOVSKIJ, P. I. 1953. The Paleolithic of the Ukraine (in Russian). *MIA*, no. 40.

BORISKOVSKIJ, P. I. 1958. The study of Paleolithic dwellings in the USSR (in Russian). *SA*, no. 1, pp. 3-19.

BORISKOVSKIJ, P. I, and PRASLOV, N. D. 1964. The Paleolithic of the Dnepr basin and the Priazov'e (in Russian). *Svod arkheologicheskikh istochnikov* A 1-5. Moscow and Leningrad: AN SSSR.

BOSINSKI, G. 1967. Die mittelpaläolithischen Funde im westlichen Mitteleuropa. In *Fundamenta*, series A, vol. 4. Cologne.

BOTEZ, I. G. 1933. Recherches de paléontologie humaine au nord de la Bessarabie. *Annales scientifiques de l'Université de Jassy* 17:397-471.

BRACE, C. L. 1964. The fate of the "classic" Neanderthals: A consideration of hominid catastrophism. *Current Anthropology* 5:3-46.

BRACE, C. L. 1966. Comment in *Current Anthropology* 7:37-38.

BRACE, C. L. 1967. *The stages of human evolution.* Englewood Cliffs: Prentice-Hall.

BROTHWELL, D. R. 1960. Upper Pleistocene human skull from Niah Caves, Sarawak. *Sarawak Museum Journal* 9:323-49.

BUD'KO, V. D. 1964. About the dwellings of the Berdyzh Paleolithic site (in Russian). *KSIA* 101:31-34.

BUD'KO, V. D. 1966. Sites of the Swiderian-Grensk culture on the territory of Belorussia (in Russian). *MIA* 126:35-46.

BUD'KO, V. D. 1967. The Yudinovo Upper Paleolithic settlement (in Russian). *AO 1966 g.* pp. 27-29.

BUD'KO, V. D. 1968. The Upper Paleolithic site of Studenets (in Russian). *AO 1967 g.* p. 244.

BUD'KO, V. D., and SOROKINA, S. A. 1969. The Upper Paleolithic of the northwest part of the Russian plain (in Russian). In *PIRPO*, pp. 127-36.

BUD'KO, V. D.; VOZNYACHUK, L. N.; and KALEGETS, E. G. 1971. The Paleolithic site of Berdyzh (in Russian). *AO 1970 g.* pp. 303-4.

BUD'KO, V. D.; VOZNYACHUK, L. N.; and KOCHETKOV, V. I. 1970. Some results of the excavations of the Berdyzh site (in Russian). *AO 1969 g.* pp. 295-96.

BURTON, M. 1962. *Systematic dictionary of the mammals of the world.* London: Musèum Press Ltd.

BUTZER, K. W. 1967. Last Glacial tundra vegetation in central Europe. *Geographical Review* 57:264-65.

BUTZER, K. W. 1971. *Environment and archeology.* Rev. ed. Chicago: Aldine.

CHARD, C. S. 1969. Archeology in the Soviet Union. *Science* 163:774-79.

CHERDYNSTEV, V. V.; ALEKSEEV, V. A.; KIND, N. V.; FOROVA, V. S.; ZAVEL'SKIJ, F. S.; SULERZHITSKIJ, L. D.; and CHURIKOVA, I. V. 1965. Radiocarbon dates of the laboratory of the Geological Institute of the AN SSSR (in Russian). *Geokhimiya,* no. 12, pp. 1410-22.

CHERDYNTSEV, V. V.; ZAVEL'SKIJ, F. S.; KIND, N. V.; SULERZHITSKIJ, L. D.; and FOROVA, V. S. 1969. Radiocarbon dates of the Geological Institute of the AN SSSR IV (in Russian). *BKICP* 36:172-93.

CHERNYSH, A. P. 1953. The Vladimirovka Paleolithic site (in Russian). *BKICP* 17:43-51.

CHERNYSH, A. P. 1959. The Upper Paleolithic of the middle Dnestr region (in Russian). *TKICP* 15:5-214.

CHERNYSH, A. P. 1961. *The Paleolithic site of Molodova V* (in Ukranian). Kiev: AN Ukr. SSR.

CHERNYSH, A. P. 1965. The Lower and Middle Paleolithic of the Dnestr region (in Russian). *TKICP*, no. 25.

CHERNYSH, A. P. 1968a. The Paleolithic site of Ataki I in the Dnestr region (in Russian). *BKICP* 35:102-12.

CHERNYSH, A. P. 1968b. Excavations at Oselivka (in Russian). *AO 1967 g.* pp. 202-3.

CHERNYSH, A. P. 1969. Investigations at Oselivka on the Dnestr (in Russian). *AO 1968 g.* pp. 266-67.

CHERNYSH, A. P. 1970. Investigations at Korman on the Dnestr (in Russian). *AO 1969 g.* pp. 220-21.

CHERNYSH, A. P. 1971a. Investigations of the multilevel site of Korman' IV in 1970 (in Russian). In *Tezisy dokladov posvyashchennykh itogam polevykh arkheologicheskikh issledovanij v 1970 godu v SSSR*, pp. 21-22. Tiflis: Metsniereba.

CHERNYSH, A. P. 1971b. Investigations of the site of Oselivka I in 1966-1967 (in Russian). *KSIA* 126:68-77.

CHEYNIER, A. 1963. Le Périgordien n'est qu'une théorie. *Bulletin de la Société historique et archéologique du Périgord.*

CHMIELEWSKI, W. 1965. Archeological cultures of the Upper Pleistocene in Poland (in Russian). *SPPVTE*, pp. 15-23.

CLARK, J. G. D. 1967. *The Stone Age Hunters.* New York: McGraw-Hill.

COLLINS, D. 1969. Culture traditions and environment of early man. *Current Anthropology* 10:267-316.

COOPE, G. R., and SANDS, C. H. S. 1966. Insect faunas of the last glaciation from the Tame Valley, Warwickshire. *Proceedings of the Royal Society*, series B. 165:389-412.

COPELAND, L. 1970. The early Upper Paleolithic flint material from levels VII-V, Antelias Cave, Lebanon. *Berytus* (Archeological Studies) 19:99-143.

DAVID, A. I. 1969. New discoveries of remains of Anthropogene mammals on the territory of Moldavia (in Russian). In *Antropogen Moldavii*, pp. 3-17. Kishinev: AN Mold. SSR.

DAVID, A. I., and KETRARU, N. A. 1970. The mammal fauna of the Moldavian Paleolithic (in Russian). *Fauna Kajnozoja Moldavii*, pp. 3-52. Kishinev: AN Mold. SSR.

DENTON, G. H.; ARMSTRONG, R. L.; and STUIVER, M. 1971. The late Cenozoic glacial history of Antarctica. In *Late Cenozoic Glacial Ages*, ed. K. Turekian, pp. 267-306. New Haven: Yale University Press.

EFIMENKO, P. P. 1953. *Primeval Society* (in Russian). Kiev: AN Ukr. SSR.

FEJFAR, O. 1969. Human remains from the early Pleistocene in Czechoslovakia. *Current Anthropology* 10:170-73.

FINK, J. 1962. Die Gliederung des Jungpleistozäns in Österreich. *Mitteilungen der Geologischen Gesellschaft in Wien* 54:1-25.

FLINT, R. F. 1971. *Glacial and Quaternary Geology.* New York: John Wiley and Sons.

FLINT, V. E.; BEME, R. L. KOSTIN, Yu. V.; and KUZNETSOV, A. A. 1968. *Birds of the USSR* (in Russian). Moscow: Mysl'.

FREEMAN, L. G. 1966. The nature of Mousterian facies in Cantabrian Spain. *American Anthropologist* 68 (no. 2, pt. 2):230-37.

FREEMAN, L. G. 1971. Los niveles de ocupación musteriense. In *Cueva Morín: Excavaciones 1966-1968*, ed. J. Echegaray and L. G. Freeman, pp. 25-162. Santander: Patraonato de las Cuevas Prehistóricas de la Provincia de Santander.

FRENZEL, B. 1964. Pollenanalyse von Lössen. *Eiszeitalter und Gegenwart* 15:5-39.

GÁBORI, M. 1969. The Paleolithic of Hungary (in Russian). *LPPNTSVE*, pp. 252-67.

GÁBORI-CZÁNK, V. 1970. C-14 dates of the Hungarian Paleolithic. *Acta Archaeologica Academiae Scientiarum Hungaricae* 22:3-11.

GARROD, D. A. 1951. A transitional industry from the base of the Upper Paleolithic in Palestine and Syria. *Journal of the Royal Anthropological Institute* 80:121-30.

GARROD, D. A. 1955. The Mugharet el-Emireh in lower Galilee: Type station of the Emiran industry. *Journal of the Royal Anthropological Institute* 85:1-22.

GORODTSOV, V. A. 1933. Investigation of the Timonovka Paleolithic site in 1932 (in Russian). *Vestnik AN SSSR*, no. 6, pp. 41-48.

GORODTSOV, V. A. 1934. The Timonovka Paleolithic site (in Russian). *Vestnik AN SSSR*, no. 1, pp. 61-66.

GORODTSOV, V. A. 1935. The socioeconomic structure of the ancient inhabitants of the Timonovka Paleolithic site (in Russian). *SE*, no. 3, p. 3.

GORODTSOV, V. A. 1935b. The Timonovka Paleolithic site: Results of the 1933 excavations (in Russian). *Trudy Instituta antropologii, etnografii i arkheologii AN SSSR*, no. 3.

GREKHOVA, L. V. 1966. The Upper Paleolithic site of Karachizh (in Russian). *Trudy Gosudarstvennogo istoricheskogo muzeya* vol. 40.

GREKHOVA, L. V. 1968. Excavations at Timonovka (in Russian). *AO 1967 g.*, pp. 27-28.

GREKHOVA, L. V. 1969. The Upper Paleolithic of the middle Desna basin (in Russian). *PIRPO*, pp. 88-97.

GREKHOVA, L. V., and SOROKINA, R. A. 1969. Reconnaissance near the village of Timonovka in 1965 (in Russian). *KSIA* 117:38-43.

GRICHUK, V. P. 1969a. The vegetation of the Russian plain in the Mousterian epoch (in Russian). *PIRPO*, pp. 42-53.

GRICHUK, V. P. 1969b. The vegetation of the Russian plain in the Upper Paleolithic (in Russian). *PIRPO*, pp. 58-67.

GRICHUK, V. P. 1969c. The vegetational cover of the southwestern part of the Russian plain in the Upper Pleistocene (in Russian). *LPPNTSVE*, pp. 448-58.

GRIGOR'EV, G. P. 1970. The Upper Paleolithic (in Russian). *MIA* 166:43-63.

GRISHCHENKO, M. N. 1971. On the geology of the Khotylevo Lower Paleolithic locality (in Russian). *MIA* 173:179-81.

GROMOV, V. I. 1948. The paleontological and archeological basis of the strati-
graphy of the contintental deposits of the Quaternary period in the
USSR (in Russian). *Trudy Institut geologicheskikh nauk AN SSSR,*
Vyp. 64, geologicheskaya seriya, no. 17.

GROMOV, V. I.; KRASNOV, I. I.; NIKIFOROVA, K. V.; and SHANTSER, E. V. 1969.
A scheme for subdividing the Anthropogene (in Russian). *BKICP* 36:41-45.

GULICHER, A. 1969. Pleistocene and Holocene sea level changes. *Earth Science
Reviews* 5:69-97.

GVOZDOVER, M. D. 1953. The working of bone and bone artifacts of the Avdeevo site
(in Russian). *MIA* 39:193-226.

GVOZDOVER, M. D. 1958. The Avdeevo site and its place among the sites of the
Upper Paleolithic (in Russian). Candidate's dissertation, Institut
istorii material'noj kul'tury AN SSSR.

GVOZDOVER, M. D. 1961. The specific features of the flint inventory of the
Avdeevo Paleolithic site (in Russian). *KSIA* 82:112-19.

HOWELL, F. C. 1957. The evolutionary significance of variation and varieties
of "Neanderthal" man. *Quarterly Review of Biology* 32:330-47.

HOWELL, F. C. 1965. *Early man.* New York: Time, Inc.

HOWELL, F. C. 1966. Observations on the earlier phases of the European Lower
Paleolithic. *American Anthropologist* 68 (no. 2, pt. 2):88-201.

ISAAC, G. Ll.; LEAKEY, R. E. F.; and BEHRENSMEYER, A. K.1971. Archeological
traces of early hominid activities east of Lake Rudolph, Kenya.
Science 173:1129-34.

IVANOVA, I. K. 1958. About the geological conditions of occurrence of the
site of Molodova I (Bajlova ripa) (in Russian). *BKICP* 22:122-26.

IVANOVA, I. K. 1959. The geological conditions of the occurrence of Paleolithic
sites on the middle Pridnestrov'e (in Russian). *TKICP* 15:215-78.

IVANOVA, I. K. 1960. The geology of the Mousterian settlement of Molodova I
(Bajlova ripa) on the middle Pridnestrov'e (in Russian).
BKICP 24:118-29.

IVANOVA, I. K. 1961a. The geology and fauna of the Dnestr Paleolithic and
Neolithic (in Russian). In *Voprosy geologii antropogena,* pp. 67-84.

IVANOVA, I. K. 1961b. The geology of the multilevel sites of the right
bank of the middle Dnestr (in Russian). *MVSPICP* 1:447-59.

IVANOVA, I. K. 1961c. Stratigraphy of the Molodova multilevel Paleolithic
sites on the middle Pridnestrov'e and some general questions of the
stratigraphy of the Paleolithic (in Russian). *TKICP* 18:94-108.

IVANOVA, I. K. 1962. The geology of the Molodova multilevel Paleolithic
sites on the middle Dnestr (in Russian). *Anthropozoikum* 11:197-220.

IVANOVA, I. K. 1964. Role of geological structure and paleogeographical
conditions in the dispersal of ancient man (as exemplified by the
basin of the River Dniester). *Report of the VIth International
Congress on the Quaternary,* Warsaw, 1961, Archaeological and
Anthropological Section, pp. 311-23.

IVANOVA, I. K. 1965. The stratigraphic position of the Molodova Paleolithic sites on the middle Dnestr in the light of general questions of the stratigraphy and absolute geochronology of the Upper Pleistocene of Europe (in Russian). *SPPVTE*, pp. 123-40.

IVANOVA, I. K. 1966. The stratigraphy of the Upper Pleistocene of central and eastern Europe according to data from the study of loesses (in Russian). In *Verkhnij Plejstotsen*, pp. 32-66. Moscow: Nauka.

IVANOVA, I. K. 1968. The geological structure of the region of the Paleolithic site of Ataki I on the middle Pridnestrov'e (in Russian). *BKICP* 35:113-19.

IVANOVA, I. K. 1969a. Middle Pridnestrov'e (geological history): Geomorphology and paleogeography of the Pridnestrov'e in the Paleolithic (in Russian). *PIRPO*, pp. 24-27, 111-19.

IVANOVA, I. K. 1969b. The geological structure of the valley of the River Dnestr in the region of the Mousterian locality of Stinka (in Russian). *BKICP* 36:129-36.

IVANOVA, I. K. 1969c. Etude géologique des gisements Paléolithiques de l'U.R.S.S. *L'Anthropologie* 73:5-48.

IVANOVA, I. K. 1969d. Geological conditions of occurrence of the Paleolithic on the territory of the USSR (in Russian). *BMOIP* (otdel geologicheskij) 44(no. 3):18-41.

IVANOVA, I. K., and CHERNYSH, A. P. 1965. The Paleolithic site of Molodova V on the middle Dnestr (USSR). *Quaternaria* 7:197-217.

JONG, J. D. de. 1967. The Quaternary of the Netherlands. In *The Quaternary*, ed. K. Rankama, 2:301-426. New York: John Wiley and Sons.

KETRARU, N. A. 1969. Investigation of the Paleolithic in Moldavia: Brief overview of discoveries and excavations (in Russian). *Izvestiya AN Mold. SSR*, seriya biologicheskikh i khimicheskikh nauk, no. 2(1969), pp. 71-76.

KETRARU, N. A., and POLEVOJ, L. L. 1971. *Moldavia from the Stone Age to the Bronze Age* (in Russian). Kishinev: Shtiintsa.

KIND, N. V. 1969. Questions of the synchronization of geological events and climatic fluctuations in the Upper Anthropogene (in Russian). In *Osnovnye problemy geologii antropogena Evrazii*, pp. 21-35. Moscow: Nauka.

KLEIN, R. G. 1965. The Middle Paleolithic of the Crimea. *Arctic Anthropology* 3, no. 1:34-68.

KLEIN, R. G. 1966a. The Mousterian of European Russia. Ph.D. Dissertation, University of Chicago.

KLEIN, R. G. 1966b. Chellean and Acheulean on the territory of the Soviet Union. *American Anthropologist* 68, no. 2, pt 2:1-45.

KLEIN, R. G. 1967. Radiocarbon dates on occupation sites of Pleistocene age in the U.S.S.R. *Arctic Anthropology* 4:224-26.

KLEIN, R. G. 1969a. Mousterian cultures in European Russia. *Science* 165:257-65.

KLEIN, R. G. 1969b. *Man and culture in the late Pleistocene: A case study*. San Francisco: Chandler Pub. Co.

KLEIN, R. G. 1970. The Mousterian of European Russia. *Proceedings of the Prehistoric Society* 25: 77-112.

KLEIN, R. G. 1971. The Pleistocene prehistory of Siberia. *Quaternary Research* 1:133-61.

KLEIN, R. G. 1972. The late Quaternary fauna of Nelson Bay cave, Cape Province, South Africa: Its implications for cultural and environmental change and megafaunal extinctions. *Quaternary Research* 2:135-42.

KLEIN, R. G.; IVANOVA, I. K., and DEBETS, G. F. 1971. U.S.S.R. In *Catalogue of fossil hominids*, ed. K. P. Oakley, B. Campbell, and T. Molleson, vol. 2, Europe, pp. 311-35. London: British Museum.

KOLOSOV, Yu. G. 1964. Some Upper Paleolithic sites in the area of the Dnepr rapids (Osokorovka, Dubovaya balka, Yamburg) (in Russian). Appendix 2 In *Svod arkheologicheskikh istochnikov* A 1-5. Moscow and Leningrad: AN SSSR.

KOWALSKI, K. 1967. The Pleistocene extinction of mammals in Europe. In *Pleistocene extinctions*, ed. P. S. Martin and H. E. Wright, pp. 349-65. New Haven: Yale University Press.

KRETZOI, M., and VERTÉS, L. 1965. Upper Biharian (Intermindel) pebble-industry occupational site in western Hungary. *Current Anthropology* 6, no. 1: 74-87.

KURTÉN, B. 1968. *Pleistocene mammals of Europe*. London: Weidenfeld and Nicolson.

LEAKEY, R. E. F.; BUTZER, K. W.; and DAY, M. 1969. Early *Homo sapiens* remains from the Omo River region of south-west Ethiopia. *Nature* 222:1132-38.

LEROI-GOURHAN, A. 1958. Etude des restes humains fossiles provenant des grottes d'Arcy-sur-Cure (Yonne). *Annales de Paléontologie* 44:85-148.

LEROI-GOURHAN, A. 1965. Le Châtelperronien: Problème ethnologique. In *Miscelánea en Homenaje al Abate Henri Breuil*, ed. E. Ripoll Perelló, 2:75-82. Barcelona: Diputación Provincial de Barcelona.

LUMLEY, H. de, ed. 1969. Une cabane acheuléene dans la grotte du Lazaret (Nice). *Memoires de la Société préhistorique française*, 7:1-235.

LYNCH, T. F. 1966. The "Lower Périgordian" in French archaeology. *Proceedings of the Prehistoric Society* 32:156-98.

MARSHACK, A. 1972. *The roots of civilization*. New York: McGraw-Hill.

MARTIN, P. S. 1967. Prehistoric overkill. In *Pleistocene Extinctions*, ed. P. S. Martin and H. E. Wright, pp. 75-120. New Haven: Yale University Press.

MESYATS, V. A. 1957. Traces of a new Upper Paleolithic site in the vicinity of Ovruch (in Russian). *KSIA AN Ukr. SSR* 7:3-4.

MIROV, N. T. 1951. *Geography of Russia*. New York: John Wiley and Sons.

MOSKVITIN, A. I. 1966. The central European "Gottweig" and "Paudorf" and their place in the stratigraphy of the Upper Pleistocene of the European part of the USSR (in Russian). In *Verkhnij Plejstotsen*, pp. 74-92. Moscow: Nauka.

MOROZOVA, T. D. 1969a. Fossil soils of the Mousterian epoch (Mikulino Interglacial) of the Central part of the Russian plain (in Russian). *PIRPO*, pp. 53-58.

MOROZOVA, T. D. 1969b. The soil cover of the Russian plain in the early time of the Upper Paleolithic (in Russian). *PIRPO*, pp. 67-69.

MOROZOVA, T. D. 1969c. Upper Pleistocene fossil soils (in Russian). *LPPNTSVE*, pp. 438-48.

MOTUZ, V. M. 1967. Quaternary molluscs from the Khotylevo Lower Paleolithic locality in Bryansk *oblast'* (in Russian). *BKICP* 33:150-54.

MOVIUS, H. L. 1949. Old World Palaeolithic archaeology. *Bulletin of the American Geological Society* 60:1943-56.

MOVIUS, H. L., Jr. 1966. The hearths of the Upper Périgordian and Aurignacian horizons at the Abri Pataud, Les Eyzies (Dordogne), and their possible significance. *American Anthropologist* 68, no. 2, pt. 2:296-325.

MOVIUS, H. L., Jr. 1969. The Châtelperronian in French archaeology: The evidence of Arcy-sur-Cure. *Antiquity* 43:111-23.

MOVIUS, H. L., Jr.; DAVID, N. C.; BRICKER, H. M.; and CLAY, R. B. 1968. The analysis of certain major classes of Upper Paleolithic tools. *Bulletin of the American School of Prehistoric Research*, no. 26.

MUSIL, R. and VALOCH, K. 1968. Stránska skála: Its meaning for Pleistocene studies. *Current Anthropology* 9:534-39.

OAKLEY, K. P.; CAMPBELL, B. G.; and MOLLESON, T. I., eds. 1971. *Catalogue of fossil hominids*, vol. 2, Europe. London: British Museum.

PALMA DI CESNOLA, A. 1966. Il paleolitico superiore arcaico (facies uluziana) della Grotta del Cavallo, Lecce. *Rivista di Scienze Prehistoriche* 21, no. 1:3-59.

PETRICHENKO, N. F. 1961. Investigation of the Upper Paleolithic site of Zamost'e I (in Russian). *BKICP* 26:153-57.

PETRICHENKO, N. F. 1963. The Upper Paleolithic site of Bila on the Prut (in Russian). *SA*, no. 3, pp. 215-18.

PEVZNER, M. A. 1970. Paleomagnetic studies of Pliocene-Quaternary deposits of the Pridnestrovie. *Palaeogeography, Palaeoclimatology, Palaeoecology* 8:215-19.

PIDOPLICHKO, I. G. 1969. *Upper Paleolithic mammoth bone dwellings in the Ukraine* (in Russian). Kiev: Naukova dumka.

PILBEAM, D. 1972. *The ascent of man*. New York: Macmillan.

POLIKARPOVICH, K. M. 1968. The Paleolithic of the Upper Podneprov'e (in Russian). Minsk: AN Belorus. SSR.

REED, C. A. 1970. Extinction of mammalian megafauna in the Old World late Quaternary. *BioScience* 20:284-88.

ROGACHEV, A. N. 1953. Investigation of the remains of a primitive communal settlement of Upper Paleolithic time near the village of Avdeevo on the Sejm in 1949 (in Russian). *MIA* 39:137-91.

ROGACHEV, A. N. 1964. Paleolithic dwellings and settlements in eastern Europe. Paper presented to the 7th International Congress of Anthropological and Ethnographic Sciences, Moscow, August 1964.

ROGACHEV, A. N. 1970. About the relative antiquity, geological and absolute age of the Paleolithic sites of the Russian plain (in Russian). In *Periodizatsiya i geokhronologiya plejstotsena,* pp. 111-13. Leningrad: Geograficheskoe obshchestvo Soyuza SSR.

SACKETT, J. R. 1966. Quantitative analysis of Upper Paleolithic stone tools. *American Anthropologist* 68 (2, 2):356-94.

SACKETT, J. R. 1968. Method and theory in Upper Paleolithic archeology in southwest France. In *New perspectives in archaeology,* ed. S. R. Binford and L. R. Binford. Chicago: Aldine.

SAHLINS, M. D. 1968. *Tribesmen.* Englewood Cliffs, N.J.: Prentice-Hall.

SAVICH, V. P. 1968. Investigation of the Upper Paleolithic site of Lipa I on the Volyn' (in Russian). *AO 1967 g.,* pp. 203-4.

SAVICH, V. P. 1969a. Bone artIfacts from the site of Lipa VI (in Russian). *BKICP* 36:136-41.

SAVICH, V. P. 1969b. Investigations of the Upper Paleolithic site of Kulychivka (in Russian). *AO 1968 g.,* pp. 262-63.

SAVICH, V. P. 1971. Investigations of the Podolian Paleolithic expedition (in Russian). *AO 1970 g.,* 231-32.

SEEMENOV, S. A. 1964. *Prehistoric technology.* Translated from the Russian by M. W. Thompson. New York: Barnes and Noble.

SEMENTSEV, A. A.; ROMANOVA, E. N.; and DOLUKHANOV, P. M. 1969. Radiocarbon dates of the laboratory of the LOIA (in Russian). *SA,* no. 1, pp. 251-61.

SERGEEV, G. P. 1950. The Upper Acheulean site in the cave near the village of Vykhvatintsy, Moldavia (in Russian). *SA* 12:203-12.

SERVICE, E. R. 1966. *The Hunters.* Englewood Cliffs, N. J.: Prentice-Hall.

SERVICE, E. R. 1971. *Primitive Social Organization.* New York: Random House.

SHOVKOPLYAS, I. G. 1965a. The Radomyshl' site: Evidence of the beginning time of the Upper Paleolithic (in Russian). *SPPVTE,* pp. 104-16.

SHOVKOPLYAS, I. G. 1965b. *The Mezin Site* (in Russian). Kiev: Naukova dumka.

SHOVKOPLYAS, I. G. 1967. New Upper Paleolithic site in Chernigov *oblast'* (in Russian). *AO 1966 g.,* pp. 187-89.

SHOVKOPLYAS, I. G. 1970. Excavations of the Dobranichevka site (in Russian). *AO 1969 g.,* pp. 222-23.

SHOVKOPLYAS, I. G. 1971a. Investigation of the Dobranichevka site and some questions of social orgainzation in the Upper Paleolithic epoch (in Russian). In *Tesizy dokladov posvyashchennykh itogam polevykh arkheologicheskikh issledovanij v 1970 godu v SSSR.* Tiflis: Metsniereba.

SHOVKOLPYAS, I. G. 1971b. Investigations of the Dobranichevka site (in Russian). *AO 1970 g.,* pp. 229-30.

SKINNER, J. H. 1965. The flake industries of Southwest Asia: A typological study. Ph.D. dissertation, Columbia University.

SMITH, P. E. L. 1965. Palaeolithic radiocarbon dates from southwestern Europe and the Mediterranean basin. In *Proceedings of the Sixth International Conference on Radiocarbon and Tritium Dating*, pp. 149-209.

SOLECKI, R. 1963. Prehistory in Shanidar Valley, Northern Iraq. *Science* 139: 179-93.

SOLECKI, R. 1971. *Shanidar: The first flower people*. New York: Knopf.

SONNEVILLE-BORDES, D. de. 1959. Position stratigraphique et chronologie relative des restes remains du Paléolithique supérieur entre Loire et Pyrénées. *Annales de Paléontologie* 45:19-51.

SONNEVILLE-BORDES, D. de. 1960. *Le paléolithique supérieur en Périgord*. Bordeaux: Delmas.

SONNEVILLE-BORDES, D. de. 1963. Upper Paleolithic cultures in western Europe. *Science* 142:347-55.

SONNEVILLE-BORDES, D. de, and PERROT, J. 1954-56. Lexique typologique du Paléolithique supérieur. *Bulletin de la Société préhistorique française* 51:327-35; 52:76-79; 53:408-12; 53:547-59.

STRUEVER, S. 1968. Flotation techniques for the recovery of small-scale archeological remains. *American Antiquity* 33:353-62.

THOMA, A. 1967. Human teeth from the Lower Paleolithic of Hungary. *Zeitschrift für Morphologie und Anthropologie* 58:152-80.

THOMA, A. 1969. Biometrische Studie über das Occipitale von Vértesszöllös. *Zeitschrift für Morphologie und Anthropologie* 60:229-41.

THOMA, A. and VERTES, L. 1971. Hungary. In *Catalogue of fossil hominids*, ed. K. P. Oakley, B. G. Campbell, and T. I. Molleson, Part 2, Europe, pp. 223-29. London: British Museum.

TSAPENKO, M. M.; BUD'KO, V. D.; and VOZNYACHUK, L. N. 1961. Geological conditions of the occurrence of Paleolithic sites on the territory of Belorussia (abstract) (in Russian). *TKICP* 18:72-74.

VALOCH, K. 1968. Evolution of the Paleolithic in central and eastern Europe. *Current Anthropology* 9:351-90.

VALOCH, K. 1969. The beginning of the Upper Paleolithic in central Europe (in Russian). *BKICP* 36:63-74.

VALOCH, K. 1971. Les paléolithiques inférieur et moyen en Europe centrale. In *Actes du VIIIe Congrès International des Sciences prehistoriques et protohistoriques*, 1:27-40. Belgrade.

VANDERMEERSCH, B. 1969. Les nouveaux squelettes moustériens découverts à Qafzeh (Israël) et leur signification. *Comptes Rendus de l'Academie des Sciences* (Paris) 268:2562-65.

VEKILOVA, E. A. 1971. The Stone Age of the Crimea (in Russian). *MIA* 173:117-61.

VEKLICH, M. F. 1961. Genetic types and lithological composition of the Quaternary deposits of the right bank of the middle Dnepr (in Russian). *MVSPICP* 2:147-53.

VELICHKO, A. A. 1961a. *The Geological age of the Upper Paleolithic of the central regions of the Russian plain* (in Russian). Moscow: AN SSSR.

VELICHKO, A. A. 1961b. About the possibilities of geological comparison of the regions of the paleolithic sites in the basins of the Desna and Don and on the territory of Czechoslovakia (in Russian). *TKICP* 18:50-61.

VELICHKO, A. A. 1969a. The basin of the upper and middle Dnepr (in Russian). The Paleogeography of Upper Paleolithic sites in the middle Dnepr basin (in Russian). *PIRPO*. pp. 22-24, 97-103.

VELICHKO, A. A. 1969b. The development of frost processes in the Upper Pleistocene (in Russian). *LPPNTSVE*, pp. 429-38.

VELICHKO, A. A., and MOROZOVA, T. D. 1969. Basic features of the paleogeography of the Russian Plain in the Upper Pleistocene (in Russian). *LPPNTSVE*, pp. 458-65.

VERESHCHAGIN, N. K. 1967. Primitive hunters and Pleistocene extinctions in the Soviet Union. In *Pleistocene Extinctions*, ed. P. S. Martin and H. E. Wright, pp. 365-98. New Haven: Yale University Press.

VÉRTES, L. 1964. *Tata, eine mittelpaläolithische Travertin-Siedlung in Ungarm*. Budapest: Akadémiai Kiadó.

VÉRTES, L. 1965a. Typology of the Buda industry, a pebble-tool Industry from the Hungarian Lower Paleolithic. *Quaternaria* 7:185-95.

VÉRTES, L. 1965b. An essay in the investigation of the Mousterian-Upper Paleolithic transition using Hungarian material (in Russian). *SPPVTE*, pp. 24-27.

VINOGRADOV, A. P.; DEVIRTS, A. L.; DOBKINA, E. I.; and MARKOVA, N. G. 1962. Determination of absolute age according to C-14 (communication 3) (In Russian). *Geokhimiya*, no. 5, pp. 387-402.

VOGEL, J. C. 1966. Comment in *Current Anthropology* 7:46-47.

VOGEL, J. C., and WATERBOLK, H. T. 1963. Groningen radiocarbon dates IV. *Radiocarbon* 5:163-202.

VOGEL, J. C., and WATERBOLK, H. T. 1967. Groningen radiocarbon dates VIII. *Radiocarbon* 9:107-55.

VOGEL, J. C., and WATERBOLK, H. T. 1972. Groningen radiocarbon dates X. *Radiocarbon* 14 (no. 1):6-110.

WATKINS, N. D. 1972. Review of the development of the geomagnetic polarity time scale and discussion of prospects for its finer definition. *Geological Society of America Bulletin* 83:551-74.

WEST, R. G. 1967. The Quaternary of the British Isles. In *The Quaternary*, Vol. 2, ed. K. Rankama, pp. 1-88. New York: John Wiley and Sons.

WEST, R. G. 1968. *Pleistocene geology and biology*. New York: John Wiley and Sons.

WOLDSTEDT, P. 1967. The Quaternary of Germany. In *The Quaternary*, vol. 2, ed. K. Rankama, pp. 239-300. New York: John Wiley and Sons.

WOLPOFF, M. H. 1971. Is Vértesszöllös II an occipital of European *Homo erectus*? *Nature* 232:567-68.

ZAGWIJN, W.; VAN MONTFRANS, H. M.; and ZANDSTRA, J. G. 1971. Subdivision of the "Cromerian" in the Netherlands: Pollen-analysis, palaeomagnetism, and sedimentary petrology. *Geologie en Mijnbouw* 50:41-58.

ZAGWIJN, W., and PAEPE, R. 1968. Die Stratigraphie der weichselzeitlichen Ablagerungen der Niederlande und Belgiens. *Eiszeitalter und Gegenwart* 19:129-46.

ZAMYATNIN, S. N. 1929. Expedition for the study of paleolithic culture in 1927 (in Russian). *Soobshcheniya Gosudarstvennoj akademii istorii material'noj kul'tury* 2:209-14.

ZAMYATNIN, S. N. 1940. The first discovery of the paleolithic in the valley of the Sejm (in Russian). *KSIIMK* 7:96-101.

ZAVERNYAEV, F. M. 1961. *The Khotylevo Lower Paleolithic locality* (in Russian). Bryansk: Bryansk Oblast' Museum.

ZAVERNYAEV, F. M. 1970. A new Upper Paleolithic site in the region of the city of Bryansk (in Russian). *AO 1969 g.*, pp. 44-45.

ZAVERNYAEV, F. M. 1971. The Lower Paleolithic locality near the village of Khotylevo on the Desna (in Russian). *MIA* 173:173-78.

ZAVERNYAEV, F. M., and SHMIDT, E. A. 1961. A new find of the Lower Paleolithic on the upper Desna (in Russian). *SA*, no. 1, pp. 243-47.